THE
PATIENCE
OF
GOD

THE
PATIENCE
OF
GOD

Rev. Valentino Del Mazza, S.D.B.

ST. PAUL EDITIONS

NIHIL OBSTAT:
 Rev. Timothy J. Shea
 Censor

IMPRIMATUR:
 ✠ Bernard Cardinal Law
 Archbishop of Boston

Library of Congress Cataloging in Publication Data

Del Mazza, Valentino.
 The patience of God.

 Translation of: La pazienza di Dio.
 1. God—Patience. 2. Patience—Religious aspects—Christianity. I. Title.
BT153.P36D4513   1984   231'.4   84-26011

ISBN 0-8198-5820-X c
 0-8198-5821-8 p

Cover Credit: V. Mancusi

Printed in the U.S.A., by the Daughters of St. Paul 50 St. Paul's Ave., Boston, MA 02130

The Daughters of St. Paul are an international congregation of women religious serving the Church with the communications media.

CONTENTS

*Every once in a while
our fragile human bark
gets new impetus
on its way toward the shores
of hope and of love;
even without realizing it
we catch a new glimpse
of the meaning of life.*

*With this book on the "patience of God,"
I, too, humbly but enthusiastically
want to give my little pull
on the oars in that direction,
particularly for the benefit
of afflicted persons.*

THE AUTHOR

Preface

The Patience of God by Father Valentino Del Mazza is a splendid book that cried out to be translated from the Italian and brought to the attention of American readers. It is an outstanding spiritual work where the theology is sound and the knowledge of the Scriptures and the Fathers of the Church profound, while there is a wealth of illustration from sources both ecclesiastical and secular.

We know that God is All-Being ("I am Who am"), but that the divinity is reflected however imperfectly in all else that has being, including virtues. With outstanding insight Father Valentino traces that reflection in patience, and he follows the thinking on this through the Bible, the Doctors of the Church and other ecclesiastical as well as secular writers, contributing also his own moving reflections.

Preachers will find the book not only an inspiration for their own spiritual development, but a treasury of sermon material. Religious and laity seeking to advance in the spiritual life will be enlightened, inspired, consoled and motivated. It is a book filled with fresh insights into an initially startling idea that patience can be attributed not only to man but to God, and that it can be a pivotal virtue in the creature's road to holiness.

I think every reader will acknowledge a debt of gratitude not only to Father Valentino but to the Daughters of St. Paul for making the book available. It is an exceptional work to be enthusiastically recommended.

—Rev. James P. Kelleher
St. Ambrose College
Davenport, Iowa

The Divine Patience

It is very difficult to express God adequately. An ancient prayer of the Bambemba (an African tribe) sheds some light on this fact:

Before things began, God exists.
God exists today, God will exist tomorrow.
But who can picture God to himself?
He has no body.
He is like a word you pronounce with your
  lips.
That word belongs to the past, but it still
  lives.
Such is God.

God is Trinity: Father, Son, and Holy Spirit. As Incarnate Son, He is "God-with-us," Emmanuel; as Holy Spirit, He is "God-in-us"; but as Father, God remains outside us, external to our every sense experience: He is totally Other. As a Being infinitely different from us, God will remain for our minds a mysterious, hidden God (cf. Dt. 5:22; 31:17; Is.

45:15; 64:7). We know, further, that it is precisely the Father who is the beginning and the source of every blessing and of our salvific history. Now if—as the ancients already said—activity follows from being, it is likewise true that the manner, the style of God's activity and His goodness can elude our manner of thinking and acting. Scripture assures us that we shall always be constitutionally incapable of determining the countenance of God (cf. Dt. 4:12; Jb. 41:1 Douay); the ways of God are not our ways, they are not the ways of finite and earthly beings (cf. Is. 55:8; Rom. 11:33).

Despite this fact, we firmly believe that God is patience, even though—as Sacred Scripture continually cautions us—He is also supreme justice (cf. Dt. 32:4; Jb. 37:23; Wis. 1:15; Am. 5:24; Acts 7:7). We believe and confidently confess all this because the Lord Himself has repeatedly told us so!

Among the many descriptions of divinity handed down to us in Sacred Scripture we find this one: "God is patient and merciful." In fact, this very expression is the leit-motif of the whole Bible, from the book of Genesis to Revelation.

The Patience of the Father

In this first chapter we shall limit ourselves to reflecting on the patience of the Father portrayed in the history of the Covenant He made with the Hebrew people.

From all eternity God has had a design of love and friendship with His creatures. This design of communion, present and active already from the beginning of human history in the terrestrial garden, was unfortunately shattered by the refusal of love on the part of Adam and Eve, official representatives of humanity. But the Lord, whose designs of benevolence never remain unaccomplished, takes up again with infinite patience the severed strands of the broken friendship, and begins to refashion the bond for the benefit and glory of the very creatures who betrayed Him. It is the Lord who seeks out the man: "Adam, where are you?" the Lord asks (Gn. 3:9). In the biblical sense, "to seek" is synonymous with "to love," to win back again with infinite patience the person beloved.

After the first failure and then the catastrophe of the flood, the Lord said to Noah:

"Behold, I establish my covenant with you and your descendants after you, and with every living creature that is with you.... I set my bow in the cloud, and it shall be a sign of the covenant between me and the earth.... The waters shall never again become a flood to destroy all flesh" (Gn. 9:9-15).* This is the promise and the universal alliance: God wills to extend His benevolence for all time upon humanity, offering His love for all generations. At its apex the rainbow touches the heavens, the realm of God, while its two extremities rest upon the earth, the fatherland of men, to indicate a pact of love between divinity and humanity, cosmic in its dimensions, total and eternal.

For God to insert Himself into this wonderful and exalting design of reconciliation and communion with creatures implies an infinite and persistent patience in supporting and remedying all the infidelities of Israel. In the creation of heaven and earth the activity of the Lord followed a gentle and progressive rhythm; in the history of the Covenant, however, the Creator has to act with much indulgence, with great patience and power of persuasion.

In the story of Abraham we see how the Lord clearly makes evident His patience and

His perduring search for man, even to the point of making a nuptial pact with him. God initiates the relationship. Befitting the social milieu of the time, He picks out a tribal chief, Abram, through whom He wills to form a people united to Him in the bonds of friendship; through this people, then, He wills to regain the friendship of the whole of humanity. Abram is called to leave his land, to become the friend of God, to experience that this God knows how to wait, how to be patient and conciliating even to the point of seeming ready to annul His divine justice (cf. dialogue on the destruction of Sodom and Gomorrah (Gn. 18:16-33).

By the time of Moses, the partners in the Covenant dialogue are God and the people. The event of Sinai constitutes the fundamental moment of the whole life of Israel, now involved in the joyful experience of a God who is all love and tenderness. What are the forty years of wandering in the desert but a continuous manifestation of the condescension of the Lord toward a stiff-necked people? Moses himself, aware of this condescension, took advantage of this "weaker side" of God to invoke Him in the name of His mercy and patience to avert the merited punishment for the sinful happenings on the journey to the Promised Land. Sacred Scripture tells us that Moses once pleaded with the Lord: "O Lord, why does your wrath burn hot against your people, whom you have brought forth out of the land of Egypt with great power and with a mighty hand?... Turn from your fierce wrath, and repent of this evil against your people...." The text continues: "And the Lord repented of the evil which he thought to do to his people" (Ex. 32:11-14).*

In the eighth century before Christ this Covenant acquires a new ethic coloring: it becomes more profound. The theologian of this new relationship between God and the Hebrews is Hosea. At the time of this prophet the Assyrians were threatening and gradually conquering the northern kingdom of Israel, while within the kingdom there were rebellions, riotings, and violence. And precisely in this historical turmoil, without hope and without peace, Hosea presents and preaches God as a lover in search of the people He loves. The son of Beeri—that was the name of Hosea's father—speaks to his fellow citizens in ardent terms to convince them that the Most High, far from retracting His pact of alliance, is rather calling His people more intimately to Himself to enfold them in a sweet and patient love such as unites husband and wife. The Lord says: "I will heal their faithlessness; I will love them freely" (Hos. 14:4).*

> It was I who taught Ephraim to walk,
> I took them up in my arms;

but they did not know that I healed
    them.
I led them with cords of compassion,
    with the bands of love,
and I became to them as one
    who eases the yoke on their jaws,
    and I bent down to them and fed them.
"So you, by the help of your God, return,
    hold fast to love and justice,
    and wait continually for your God."
                          (Hos. 11:3-4; 12:6)*

It becomes the task of Jeremiah to
amplify the qualities of this new alliance
which is based upon love and interiority,
while on God's part the constant of patience
remains. "I will put my law within them,"
says Yahweh through Jeremiah, "and I will
write it upon their hearts; and I will be their
God, and they shall be my people.... Is
Ephraim my dear son? Is he my darling
child? For as often as I speak against him, I
do remember him still. Therefore my heart
yearns for him; I will surely have mercy on
him.... I have loved you with an everlasting
love" (Jer. 31:33, 20, 3).*

These expressions in their turn bring us
to the well-known assurances God has given
us through the prophet Isaiah:

Can a woman forget her sucking child,
    that she should have no compassion on
        the son of her womb?
Even these may forget,

> yet I will not forget you.
> Behold, I have graven you on the palms of
>   my hands.   (Is. 49:15-16)*
> At the favorable time I will answer you,
> On the day of salvation I will help you.
>   (Is. 49:8)

The prophet Daniel, too, consoles us with the thought of God's kindness as he addresses Him in prayer: "Do not disappoint us; treat us gently, as you yourself are gentle and very merciful" (Dn. 3:42).

If we were to select other Old Testament expressions extolling the goodness and patience of the Lord, we would find ourselves quite frustrated in the choosing for they are numerous and repetitious. The proclamation of the patience of God which we already noted in the book of Exodus: "Yahweh, Yahweh, a God of tenderness and compassion, slow to anger, rich in kindness and faithfulness..." (Ex. 34:7), resounds again and again; it is actualized and disseminated with enthusiasm and fidelity, and it recurs in variant phrasing in book after book, so much so that it can be called the dominant theme of all biblical literature. This is particularly apparent in the psalms, Israel's hymns that praise in a highly poetic and effective manner the eternal patience of God (cf. Ps. 25; 40:11-12; 41; 62; 69:14; 78:38-39; 86:3-5; 107; 118; 147; etc.), in which:

Love and loyalty now meet,
Righteousness and Peace now embrace.
(Ps. 85:10)

Passages from two of these very expressive songs of praise will illustrate their beauty. We sing in Psalm 103:

Bless the Lord, O my soul,
  and forget not all his benefits,
who forgives all your iniquity,
  who heals all your diseases,
who redeems your life from the Pit,
  who crowns you with steadfast love and
    mercy....
The Lord is merciful and gracious,
  slow to anger and abounding in steadfast
    love.
He will not always chide,
  nor will he keep his anger for ever.
He does not deal with us according to our
    sins,
  nor requite us according to our iniquities.
As a father pities his children,
  so the Lord pities those who fear him.*

In Psalm 136 the praise of the Lord is explosive:

O give thanks to the Lord, for he is good,
  for his steadfast love endures for ever.
O give thanks to the God of gods,
  for his steadfast love endures for ever.
O give thanks to the Lord of lords,
  for his steadfast love endures for ever;

to him who alone does great wonders,
   for his steadfast love endures for ever;
to him who by understanding made the
      heavens,
   for his steadfast love endures for ever;
to him who spread out the earth upon the
      waters,
   for his steadfast love endures for ever;
to him who made the great lights,
   for his steadfast love endures for ever;
the sun to rule over the day,
   for his steadfast love endures for ever;
the moon and stars to rule over the night,
   for his steadfast love endures for ever....

It is he who remembered us in our low
      estate,
   for his steadfast love endures for ever;
and rescued us from our foes,
   for his steadfast love endures for ever;
he who gives food to all flesh,
   for his steadfast love endures for ever;
O give thanks to the God of heaven,
   for his steadfast love endures for ever.*

It is good to recall that this comforting
message of divine patience was proclaimed
even to the pagans, as we learn from the story
of the prophet Jonah. Despite his reluctance to
accept the mission, this prophet was charged
by God to go to Nineveh and arouse within
the hearts of the citizens there the sublime
truth that Yahweh was "a God of tenderness

and compassion, slow to anger, rich in graciousness, relenting from evil" (Jon.4:2). Let us briefly review this interesting story: The word of the Lord came to Jonah, son of Amittai: "Up! Go to Nineveh, the great city, and inform them that their wickedness has become known to me." But Jonah, suspecting that God might pardon such great evil and not sharing in God's merciful designs, tried to escape from the mission by boarding a ship bound for Tarshish, a city at the extremity of the then known world.[1] When a violent storm arose on the sea, the sailors, believing Jonah to be a sinner and therefore responsible for their being in danger of perishing, cast him into the sea. Remaining inside the fish for three days he is, as it were, constrained to make a three-day retreat. During these days of grace he prays to the Lord for salvation, and is forced to reflect upon the divine mercy he had wanted to deny unconditionally to the Ninevites. When he was finally cast out upon the shore he found himself right at Nineveh. He set about preaching zealously the threatened chastisements of God and the absolute need of penance. The people receive his message,

---

1. Tarshish is identified by some as a Greek city, by others as a city of Sicily, by still others as a city on the coast of Spain (Tartenos). This third presumption has the most probability.

and all from the smallest to the greatest, with the king at the head, begin to fast in the hope that God will be merciful and pardon them. The Lord pardons the people, but Jonah cannot suppress his indignation, his resentment at such mercy: the prophet cannot comprehend how God could be "merciful, clement, longsuffering" and change His mind about inflicting the threatened disaster. Indignant, Jonah goes away to a little shelter outside the city, but the sun scorches his head with its rays. The Lord lets a vine grow over his shelter, and this son of Amittai is delighted in the plant and his ill-humor is soothed. But during the night the vine dries up, and now Jonah openly complains against the Lord and wishes himself dead. At this point God Himself admonishes Jonah: "You pity the plant, for which you did not labor, nor did you make it grow, which came into being in a night, and perished in a night. And should not I pity Nineveh, that great city, in which there are more than a hundred and twenty thousand persons who do not know their right hand from their left, and also much cattle?" (Jon. 4:10-14)

This message of patience and mercy is propagated more extensively through the prophecy handed down to us through the book of Tobit. This sacred book, written probably about 200 B.C. in the Aramaic language, recounts a familiar story all interwoven with patience. At Nineveh there lives a man named Tobit, exiled with his tribe of Naphtali, devout, law-abiding, charitable, and now blind. At Ecbatana, at that time capital of Media and later the summer residence of the Persian kings, lives Sarah, daughter of Raguel, kinsman of Tobit. Sarah, too, has been touched by sorrow, because Asmodeus, the "wicked demon," has killed one after another of her seven bridegrooms on their wedding night. Both Tobit and Sarah, however, continue to trust patiently in the Lord: "You are just, O Lord, and just are all your works. All your ways are grace and truth..." (Tb. 3:2). And their trust is rewarded munificently. The Archangel Raphael, without revealing his identity, conducts Tobias, son of the blind Tobit, to Raguel, marries him to Sarah, and gives him a cure for his father's blindness. The story teaches us to recognize in God a compassionate and provident Friend who in His own time rewards those who do not spoil with their persistent impatience His loving designs, nor doubt His power and salvific patience.

The more we ponder and study the word of the Lord, the more weighty and palpable does this concept of "divine patience-mercy" become. It is for this reason that the later books of the Old Testament—Sirach (third

century before Christ) and Wisdom (first century before Christ)—present in a clear, luminous and recurrent manner the theme of the
goodness and patience of the Lord toward
that humanity which is always delineated in
its poverty and creature indigence.

Marginal to all these biblical texts praising the patience of the Lord, there is the task
of responding satisfactorily to an objection
which surely has arisen in our minds during
this meditation. If God is infinite goodness
and patience, why—this is the question so
many people ask with good reason—does He
punish so severely? Why, too, do we find in
the history of Israel an abundance of divine
avenging?

In our attempt to find a solution to the
question of the punishments—or rather self-
punishments—which fell upon the Chosen
People, let us keep in mind that the pastoral
tactics of God have two main purposes: one
pedagogical, the other apostolic and missionary.

The prophets themselves made every effort to convince the people that the trials of
the desert and of exile in faraway Assyria and
Babylonia had as an indirect purpose the
benefit of a more sincere and decisive return
to the authenticity of the Covenant. That is,
God permitted the chastisement so that His
people would understand better the value of

His permanent and unchangeable paternal love. We know that actually the Hebrews did improve and become more attached to their Lord every time they had to pass through the crucible of trial, whether of the desert or of slavery: this separation from their God hollowed out in their hearts a profound nostalgia, and as a result the renewed Covenant was celebrated with more joy and intimacy. We read in the psalm:

> When he slew them, they sought for him;
>   they repented and sought God earnestly.
> They remembered that God was their rock,
>   the Most High God their redeemer.
>   (Ps. 78:34-35)*

A second explanation, equally proclaimed by the Scriptures of the Old as well as the New Testament, is of a prophetic and missionary nature. It is this: It was only after they had suffered that the Hebrews could proclaim that their God is a God of patience and restoration, a God who knows how to wait with infinite and inexhaustible love. Further, only by being exiled in a strange land could the Israelites diffuse to many other nations of the world the happy message of a liberating and saving Lord (cf. Tb. 13:1-5). In this sense we can interpret positively a rather mysterious phrase which St. Paul addresses to the Christians of Rome: "God has imprisoned all men in their own disobedience only to show mercy to all mankind" (Rom. 11:32).

These thoughts would remain fruitless if they did not touch upon our own spiritual life. The basic attitude we must assume unhesitatingly is that of an unconditional faith in the goodness and patience of God. The Lord is gracious; He says of Himself:

> How can I give you up, O Ephraim!
>   How can I hand you over, O Israel!...
> My heart recoils within me,
>   my compassion grows warm and tender.
> I will not execute my fierce anger,
>   I will not again destroy Ephraim;
> for I am God and not man,
>   the Holy One in your midst,
>   and I will not come to destroy.
>   (Hos. 11:8-9)*

What is the history of our salvation? It is the providential space in time in which men are invited to experience and taste the infinite patience and goodness of their God. The Bible assures us that as the light of the sun invades the whole of creation, so does the mercy and indulgence of the living God radiate, or rather permeate with gratuitous light, the whole pathway of our brief existence.

> He has his rising on the edge of heaven,
> the end of his course in its furthest edge,
> and nothing can escape his heat.
>   (Ps. 19:6)

Prayer of
John Henry Newman

My Lord, people say that your judgments
    are severe
and your chastisements exaggerated.
But I do not think so.
The one experience I have of you, Lord,
    is your benevolence and mercy.
You have always come to my help.
Unmindful of my infidelity you have
    continued to love me, to favor me,
to comfort me, to surround me with
    your benedictions, to sustain me,
to help me make progress.

I sin against your love
    and you offer me even more.
I rebel against you and you not only
    do not turn me away,
you show yourself even more benevolent,
    gentle, understanding,
as if I had nothing to ask your pardon for,
    nothing to repent of, nothing to
        correct.
How many times I have set myself against
    you,
and you have continued to treat me as your
    dearest friend, most faithful and loyal.

O Lord! Every day is for me a new and
    sweeter call to your inexhaustible love,
your ineffable mercy!

I wish to give testimony of this to all.
I desire to tell everyone
that you are eternal and providential patience
    for my soul!

Newman, *Meditations and Devotions*
(London, 1964), p. 47

The Patience
of the Son

The benevolent deeds and advances of the Lord throughout the history of the Old Testament Covenant, His acts of longsuffering and patience are all integrated, confirmed and strengthened in Christ, the incarnation of the benignity and kindness of the Father (cf. Ti. 3:4). The heart of Jesus is the point through which passes all the love of the Trinity for humanity. In Him—Jesus— "goodness and mercy become attributes of 'patience in person,'" as Paul Valéry put it. Christ remains for all time the most beautiful hymn of all the mercy and patience on earth, if only we listen to hear it in this agitated, turbulent, impatient world.

The prophet Isaiah has already presented as a counterpart to the calculating meanness of men the patience of God in the person of the future Messiah:

Again the Lord spoke to Ahaz, "Ask a sign of the Lord your God; let it be deep as Sheol or high as heaven." But Ahaz said, "I will not ask, and I will not put the Lord to the test." And he said, "Hear then, O house of David! Is it too little for you to weary men, that you weary my God also? Therefore the Lord himself will give you a sign. Behold, a young woman shall conceive and bear a son, and shall call his name Immanuel."

(Is. 7:10-14)*

With the birth of the Incarnate Word in time, a wonderful story of divine patience is unfolded for us, a patience that is effective and timeless. Never before had such a story been heard, never before such an amazing promise given. Yet how surprising is the unfolding of the story: The One awaited by the people is not received by the people of Bethlehem; His place of birth is an abandoned cave outside the city. The Messiah comes to free men from their sin—for this reason He is given the name Jesus—yet He is constrained to flee to the land of Egypt because of the pride of a wicked king, the bloodthirsty Herod the Great, king of Judea. Jesus returns to Nazareth and chooses to live in seclusion, in the house of Joseph and Mary, obeying them and with divine patience helping them in humble chores in the home and the carpenter shop.

The patience of the Son of God shines out, too, in His public life. At His first appearance John the Baptist points Him out as a lamb, "Look, there is the lamb of God" (Jn. 1:36); He is the meek and patient lamb who must be led to death for the sins of the world (cf. Is. 53:7). He who is to feed thousands in the desert with multiplied bread and with the spiritual food of His fascinating words subjects Himself to forty days and nights of fasting and silence in a desert place, where He also sustains the insidious and spiteful attacks of Satan. Christ, incarnate Wisdom, is misunderstood or not understood by His disciples; He is thwarted and impeded by the Scribes and Pharisees; He, Creator and Lord of the world and of all things, has no fixed dwelling for His repose; and though He has every right to be obeyed and served by His Apostles, He does not disdain to wash their feet, a task slaves performed for their masters.

The unlimited patience of Christ is even more radiant in His contact with the moral and physical miseries of the people. If He has a preference, it is for the humble, the poor, the infirm, and above all for sinners. It can be said that He lived and exercised His ministry under the standard of infinite and invincible patience: to regain the lost, to heal the wounded, to revive the dead. Without doubt the strongest documentation of the patience of Jesus is His passion and death. This great drama begins with the scene of Jesus entering the city of Jerusalem: He is riding a humble beast of burden, a reminder to all that only the meek will possess the earth (cf. Mt. 5:4). Then follows a true epic of pain and patience. He who had come to earth to form a unique family remains abandoned and alone. During the dark hours of Gethsemane He might have found consolation with His favorite Apostles, but they were asleep, quite unaware of the tragedy passing through the heart of their Master. Even in such great sorrow Jesus has the strength and gentleness to accept a kiss from Judas the traitor, and to call him "friend." Instead of reproving Peter who— intimidated by the ironic insinuations of a woman—pretends not to know Him, the Lord simply looked at His Apostle without a word. Further: He who in heaven was reverenced by a multitude of angels is now here on earth villainously insulted, buffeted, stripped and despoiled of the one seamless robe which was fashioned by the sweetest of creatures, His Mother Mary. At last He arrives at the peak of His suffering—the crucifixion. Here we see Him aglow with the "perfect patience" of the Son of God. Christ supports all, accepts voluntarily the seeming failure of His man-hood with invincible dignity and meekness. The prophet Isaiah had written of Him: "Harshly dealt with, he bore it humbly, he never opened his mouth, like a lamb that is led to the slaughter-house, like a sheep that is dumb before its shearers, never opening his mouth" (53:7). Tertullian tells us: "His enemies taunted, 'Descend from the cross!' but He did not descend from it because the nature of God is patience."

After His resurrection, too, Christ is wholly a message of patience and comfort. He does not spend His time in reprisals, in glowing marks of triumph or in clamorous victory; He keeps only the marks of His passion and death, those trophies of His love. Neither does He reprove His Apostles for their cowardice, but with delicacy and clemency He wishes them peace; He confirms them in their apostolic offices and reassures them with the promise of the Holy Spirit, sending them out into the streets of the world where they are to give testimony of His love.

All this supereminent epiphany of patience on the part of the Redeemer would simply have to find resonance, as a matter of course, in His teaching. The word of Jesus was calm, penetrating, always respectful and timely. When He spoke, His gaze rested with pleasure upon the most simple symbols of nature and the wonderful views of the surrounding countryside. His voice had the transparency of eternity, the harmony of the ages, the gentleness of the dawn. It was clothed with power from on high, but it offered a colloquy that was sincere, humanly warm, affectionate, nobly patient. Whenever He had to confront His enemies He intervened without agitation, with a superb psychological finesse. His rhetorical pauses were like cosmic silences—not so much to impose His masterful supremacy or humiliate His adversaries, but rather to arouse in them a yearning for truth and to create in their hearts an urge for divine communion in the love of the Father.

Christ spoke with all. He gave His attention to the little ones, gathered around Him in joy and admiration against the will of the Apostles; when the blind man called out to Him He listened and bade him approach, despite the crowds blocking the way. Jesus spoke to women and offered them the light of truth, though at that time both law and tradition forbade them the direct teaching of a prophet. All in all, in His manner of communicating with unalterable patience the word of life, Jesus has made Himself for all time the insuperable model of dialogue.

Then if we analyze the specific content of His teaching, we note that the central theme of His words is God's loving patience toward men. One sole reference to a Gospel passage will be sufficient to substantiate this statement. One day at the order of the Master the Apostles went into a Samaritan village to make preparations for the Lord's passage. But the people would not receive Him because He was on His way to Jerusalem. James and John were outraged at their rebuff and asked, "Lord, do you want us to call down fire from heaven and burn them up?" But He rebuked their immoderate zeal, for after all the Son of Man had come not to punish but to seek and save what was lost (cf. Lk. 9:52-55; 19:10).

Let us remember, finally, that all the Gospel parables are a testimony of the long-suffering and patience of God. The story of the lost sheep (cf. Mk. 18:12-14; Lk. 15:4-7), of the barren fig tree in the vineyard (cf Lk. 13:6-9), the parables of Providence (cf Mt. 6:24-34; Lk. 12:22-32) can be regarded as cathedrals of divine patience.

The parable of the Prodigal Son, however, towers above all the others. In this story Jesus wishes to convince us for ever of the infinite goodness of the Father, sublimely manifested in His patient pardoning of a very great sinner. The account is recorded for us by St. Luke, "the scribe of the humility of Christ." According to Dante (De Monarchia), it unfolds in three acts.

Act One:
The Description of the Sin

A father had two sons. The younger one requested his portion, his inheritance, because he wanted to leave home and enjoy to the full his liberty without so many ethical restraints, so many paternal counsels. When the son had been given what he wanted, with a sense of self-confidence he departed to go far away, without a fixed goal. But hard reality followed the inebriation of adventure. After his patrimony had been squandered in disorderly and lavish living, the lad is forced to hire himself out as a swineherd for survival. For a Jew to engage in such a demeaning task as looking after these animals was an extreme humiliation, for in the Law swine were regarded as unclean (cf. Lv. 11:7; Mt. 7:6) and even those who tended them were contaminated and excommunicated. The situation was even more disastrous because of the fact that the master was avaricious, demanding, and hardhearted, and refused to the poor lad even the husks that were cast to the pigs. The trial was too much for the boy and brought him to the point of collapse, of moral and psychic prostration. This very humiliation was providential, for it released in his spirit what might be termed "the dynamic of conversion." Certainly this young person had been well educated in the family, and now his innate goodness of soul and his better judgment set him to reflection. He compared his actual situation with the earlier family life he had known at home, and he envied even the servants there because of the concern the father had for them. Then in a dramatic internal tension while reflecting on his mistake or rather his sin and also his affection for his father, the boy made the decision to humiliate himself and return to the house of his father. "I will leave this place," he said decisively, "and return to my father, for I cannot continue to live like this...."

Act Two: The Patience and Goodness of the Father

This venerable father had known no peace since his beloved son, the younger in age and in experience, had made up his mind to leave home. Day after day he gazed into the distance, as if he had been told that some day his son would come back to him. And on the day when finally he spied far down the road his own dear son coming toward the house, he did not remain there to await him with the gratifying sentiment of a victor; rather, he ran toward him, embraced him and covered him with kisses, without permitting the boy to recite the little formula of accusation which he had learned by heart, asking for readmission into the family as a simple servant. And a great feast is prepared, such as was hitherto unknown. It is not a little lamb or a goat that is killed, as for a common feast, but the fatted calf, as is done on exceptional occasions. The boy is clothed in the finest robe, reserved for outstanding occasions; a ring is placed on his finger, to mark his station as a recognized son. And the motive of all this joy is repeated again and again by the father: "This my son was dead and has returned to life; he was lost and is found again!"

Act Three:
The Incomprehension
of Those Who Believe
Themselves Righteous

The elder son, having returned from the fields and having heard the jubilation, became indignant when he discovered what it was all about. He remonstrated with his father for arranging so great a feast and so much merry-making for a son who had betrayed and disgraced him. And here St. Luke, author of the third Gospel, captures with the magic touch of a photographer and the penetration of a reporter the touching delicacy and forgiving spirit of this father. The Gospel story relates that when the aged father learned of the reaction of this older son, instead of waiting for him in the banquet hall, he went down to the courtyard and hastened to the boy who was mature in years but not in heart, and explained gently to him the motive for this feast: "My son, do not be cross, but rejoice with us. And do not believe that I am unjust. See? All that is mine is yours too. But this brother of yours who was dead has returned to life; he was lost and has been found. And furthermore, from now on he will be very dutiful because of the bitter experience he has had while far from home" (cf. Lk. 15:11-31).

The context of this parable is such that it can be defined as "the Gospel within the Gospel," the heart of the Good News. In this narrative the evangelist St. Luke has succeeded in giving us a true masterpiece in every sense. Beyond the merits of its literary elegance and the lucid style typical of the Greek language, the author of this Gospel has raised up a most beautiful monument to the patience and mercy of God, from which, in the course of centuries, generation after generation can draw confidence, hope of pardon and reconciliation. Charles Peguy, the poet of hope, comments: "Except for the person who has a heart of stone, who can listen to this parable without weeping? For two thousand years it has brought tears to very many. It has touched the most interior and most profound depths of the human heart. Of all the parables of the Lord this one has awakened the deepest echo and is the only one the sinner has not silenced in his heart." [1]

Shifting our emphasis now from the theoretical and theological plane to that of the pastoral and personal, we quickly discover a never-failing assurance. It is this: When you "have no one" (cf. Jn. 5:7), Jesus is with you; though all others should abandon you, and "it is nearly evening" (cf. Lk. 24:29), He will be your companion. If you are nearly engulfed in the hardships of life, He will vivify your spirit and bolster your courage with the assurance that there is a providence (cf. Mt. 14:25; Mk. 4:38; Lk. 8:24).

Christ will always show us pity, mercy and patience (cf. Mk. 10:47; Lk. 18:39). He will come to our help immediately when we are weak and suffering (cf. Mk. 9:24). Always and everywhere Jesus is our true Friend (cf. Jn. 15:15); He is "the fullness of our desires" (St. Augustine); He is "the answer to our problems" (St. Clement of Alexandria).

---

1. See also the very beautiful commentary of Pope John Paul II on this parable in his second encyclical, *Dives in misericordia*, nos. 5-6.

In our society with its stress on the masses, a condition which makes anonymity the rule, it is certainly most consoling to know that there is a God who acts in our favor, who is patient with us under any kind of circumstance. "Life Is Wonderful!" is the title of an old film. And so it is, if we see it in this perspective: life is beautiful when it is lived in a true and constant friendship. What is Christianity? It is the most beautiful adventure of friendship between God and man, through Christ, in the Holy Spirit.

Lord, if You are with me, I fear nothing:
 You are my light!
If You are with me, I fear no enemy:
 You fight for me.
If You are my guide I will not go astray:
 You are my way.
If You counsel me I will have no more problems,
 for You are my word and my response.
If You nourish me with love I shall not feel abandoned:
 You are communion.
If You try me I shall not fear the suffering
 because You are the song of my life.
If You make me Your apostle I shall not fear my weakness
 because You are my strength.

Lord, in the happy and serene moments of my life, be my joy.

In the moments of sorrow and oppression, be
  my hope.
In the hour of my death, be my resurrection.
With You, Lord, I shall fear nothing,
  I shall never be alone,
    for You are the Eternal.
You, Lord, are the unchanging and perfect
  Friend
    of those who love You!

The Patience
of the Holy Spirit in Souls
and in the Church

If by appropriation we describe the patience of the Father as manifest in the history of the Covenant of the Old Testament, and the patience of the Son as wonderfully resplendent in the New Testament and the work of the Redemption, we may apply to the Holy Spirit the patience exercised mysteriously and powerfully in the Church from the days of Pentecost to this our own time. This is confirmed by the evangelist St. Luke who begins his history of the Church—the Acts of the Apostles—with the miraculous descent of the Holy Spirit upon the Virgin Mary and the others gathered in the Cenacle. After this stupendous event Peter goes out to preach to the crowd for the first time, and says openly: "Men of Judea and all who dwell in Jerusalem, let this be known to you, and give ear to my words.... This is what was spoken by the prophet Joel:

> 'And in the last days it shall be, God
>   declares,
> that I will pour out my Spirit upon all flesh,
> and your sons and your daughters shall
>   prophesy,

and your young men shall see visions...
yea, and on my menservants and my
      maidservants in those days
I will pour out my Spirit; and they shall
      prophesy.
And I will show wonders in the heaven
      above
and signs on the earth beneath....
And it shall be that whoever calls on the
      name of the Lord shall be saved....' "
                              (Acts 2:17-21)

The new thing about Christianity, in contrast to all other oriental religions in which the transcendence of God is untouchable and beyond every human event and relationship, consists precisely in regarding the Lord not only as totally "Other," but also as totally "Ours," that is, as the One who acts mysteriously but efficaciously, with eternal patience, in the interior of our spirits. Reechoing a prophecy of Ezekiel, Jesus compares the Holy Spirit to water (cf. Ez. 36:25-30; Jn. 7:37-39). Water is pure, humble, modest, almost preoccupied with trying to hide itself in the earth, and yet it is this very element, a fundamental element of nature, which can secretly "change the desert into luxuriant land and transform the flour into dough and then into fragrant bread" (St. Irenaeus). The Holy Spirit is like this for our souls, for our lives, and for the history of the Church.

This hidden energy, potent and vivifying, enters into the soul in Baptism. Quite without our merit and beyond all barriers of finite and corporeal externals, we are elevated through the reality of this sacrament to the dignity of "adopted sons of God" and gifted with a supernatural "new creation" (cf. 2 Cor. 5:17). But this bestowal of new quality to our being is only a beginning: it needs to develop and mature in the three theological virtues of faith, hope and charity so that the divine image, newly-stamped and imprinted in our soul, can become transformed into an effective resemblance to God, even to becoming "the perfect Man, fully mature with the fullness of Christ himself" (Eph. 4:13).

And in truth, it is in this slow and invisible process of maturing at the supernatural level where, secretly but actively, we are gifted with "the infinite, the free and indulgent play of the perennial patience of the Holy Spirit" (St. Clement of Alexandria: *The Pedagogue*).[1]

---

1. The Fathers of the Church, particularly Saint Irenaeus (m. 200), Origen (third century), the so-called Cappadocians: St. Gregory of Nazianzen, St. Gregory of Nyssa, and others, explain Genesis 1:56 "Let us make man to our image and likeness" in this way: the *image* has something static and ontological, while the *likeness* is the spiritual and ethical result of an action. Now the passage from *being* to *acting* is determined precisely—according to them—by the presence and the work of the Holy Spirit.

At this point it is easy to turn our thoughts to the seven gifts of the Holy Spirit. As light is refracted in seven colors, and harmony resolved in seven notes, the Holy Spirit, while always remaining the one infinite Love abiding in our soul, takes on dynamic modulations in the bestowal of His vivifying gifts. The Fathers of the Church and also great theologians like Augustine and Thomas Aquinas in their delineation of the seven beatitudes and the seven petitions of the Our Father are inspired above all by Isaiah's description of the effects of the Spirit (cf. Is. 11:1-9) when they fix the number *seven* to these celestial gifts. Without compromising the inexhaustible productivity of the Spirit, it seems right to say that it is precisely the gift of His wisdom which enables us to distinguish the things of eternity from the things of time. With the gift of understanding the Spirit helps us discern what is true and what is false. With His gift of counsel we are aided to judge what we ought to do and what we ought to avoid. Another gift of the Spirit is that of fortitude through which the Christian is given a reserve of strength to face and overcome the difficulties of his life and vocation. With the Spirit's gift of true knowledge we are made docile and receptive to divine teaching, while with His gift of piety we are able to offer joyous service or *diaconia* in praising the Lord. The seventh gift, holy fear, suggests to us the respect and propriety we should have in appearing before the Lord, for though He has chosen to be intimate with us, He still retains His utter transcendence and infinite justice. Saint Augustine explains and summarizes the Holy Spirit's activity in us in this manner: "Everything good that is in us comes from the Holy Spirit, while all that is evil is our own thing.... The grace of the Holy Spirit acts in such a manner that we know what it is good to do, and knowing it, we have His strength to do it. The Holy Spirit's action in us makes us understand what must be loved, and when we love it, He gives us the strength to act according to what we believe" (*On Grace*, 12, 12).

If then we should like to indicate the supernatural effects of this Spirit, we find ourselves once again before a wonderful diagram of our bonds with heaven. If, born of the Spirit, we sense by interior instinct that Christ is truly the Son of the living God, and that the one falsehood of the world is that of not believing in His divinity, this intuition is a gift of the Spirit (cf. 1 Jn. 2:22). If we are in a position to witness in word and work that the Savior of the world is Jesus Christ, this too is the fruit of the Spirit's suggestions (cf. 1 Jn. 4:9-10). Only through the silent illumination of the Spirit are we able to perceive, by a special charism, that the love of the Lord dwells within us, that ineffable love which with inexpressible sighs gives voice and efficacy to our pleas, and makes us joyfully aware of belonging to the family of the Church. Saint Irenaeus, the holy bishop of Lyons, affirmed: "Where the Church is, there is the Holy Spirit; where the Holy Spirit is, there is the Church and grace."

The patient action of the Holy Spirit is manifest, in the third place, in the divine inspiration of the Word of God. A prophet is one who speaks in the name and under the inspiration of the Spirit of God. "The sacred writer is not made a slave of the superhuman power of the efficacious action of the Spirit; he remains integrally a free cooperator with the divine action according to his own personal talents, for it is not God's way to annul specific personal gifts even when these are utilized cooperatively in the diffusion of the message of salvation" (cf. Encyclical *Divino Afflante Spiritu*, Pius XII, 1943; *Dogmatic Constitution on Divine Revelation*, Vat. II).

With this thought in mind it is easy for us to understand and appreciate how the prophet Amos, a herdsman and cultivator of sycamores, proclaims the divine oracles with absolute fidelity to the thoughts of God, but in a manner far different from the way other prophets announce their messages. His manner, for instance, is not at all like that of Daniel, a highly cultured man of a noble family, a youth accustomed to living at the court of great kings. Likewise we find that in the New Testament the style of Paul is not that of Peter, of James or John, or of anyone else.

The forbearance of the Holy Spirit is also revealed in a highly edifying manner in the person who listens to the Word. A consistent patristic train of thought which was given considerable attention in earlier centuries, and now in recent times tends to be reaffirmed, conceives the inspiration of the sacred books not alone as the divine action in rapport with the person of the prophet, but also as the gentle and permanent influence upon the person hearing and receiving the revealed message. The sacred writer as well as the reader, the preacher as well as the listener—according to St. Gregory the Great—are all touched by the divine action, though in different ways. All come under the influence of the Spirit, for the Bible is not merely some kind of theory, a book of culture; it is specifically the Word of the Holy Spirit which continues to speak to our hearts and to operate in our wills. "It is the Spirit," St. Augustine reminds us, "which does not cease to inspire, to fill with wonder all who come in contact with the Word of the Lord." This is the reason why the

Word is always fresh, always new, as if it had just been revealed for the first time. This is why it is eternally youthful, like an inexhaustible Alpine torrent; this is why the priest, after having read the Gospel, kisses it as if he wanted to make his very own the beauty and newness of the divine thoughts.[2]

Finally, it does not seem out of place to note and emphasize that the very dogmas of the Church are like providential elaborations of the patience and condescension of the Holy Spirit. Woven and developed in the bosom of the Church, they surface in history like shafts of light shining upon a truth and setting its several facets into proper perspective. They have the providential function of protecting the Christian people from perilous religious fantasies, and at the same time they sustain and encourage these people in their pursuit of fuller conquest of the Light. Pope Paul VI explains the dogmas in the light of revealed doctrine:

> Revealed doctrine, fixed in its unmistakable content, may have further development which only he to whom Christ has given the teaching authority can authenticate. It is Newman's thesis: from a truth there can be

---

2. See also: *An Essay on the Development of Christian Doctrine*, J. H. Newman.

deduced some conclusions which makes explicit a doctrine already implicit in the treasury of faith.... This is the mission of the teaching Church, that of defending revealed doctrine, replying to the difficulties and errors that history raises with regard to faith, and discovering in its treasury hidden truths which, in the process of its spiritual experience and in the casuistry of the times, call for a new testimony (Pope Paul VI, September 29, 1976).

The *Holy Spirit* is not only the Sanctifier and the interior Friend of man; He is also the *living and life-giving principle of the Church of God.* Unless we recognize that the strength, the interior and reforming dynamism, and the guarantee of historical permanence of the Spouse of Christ, Holy Church, is precisely the Holy Spirit, we shall have to admit that we do not understand anything at all about the Church. St. Augustine tells us that what sap is to the plant, what the soul is to the body, the Holy Spirit is for the Church of God. Without the Holy Spirit, all the supernatural ideals pursued by the Church would remain a dead letter, a Utopia. If the light, strength and comfort of the Holy Spirit were lacking to the people of God, even God Himself would remain far from His creatures, Christ would be relegated to the past, the Gospel would be only a record of something that had happened, Catholic worship would be only archaism, liturgy would be only a nostalgic re-evocation of the Lord's promises, the apostolate would be reduced to social propaganda, and authority, far from being service, would become imposition. All in all, the whole of the life, history and action of the Church would be merely another one of the socio-cultural manifestations which from time to time appear on the screen of the world and then disappear forever. But the truth is that the Church is not caught up in these time-bound contingencies which find their finish in non-entity; she is perennially vivified in the salvific presence of the Holy Spirit and thus is able to act in the depth of the human heart and in the fabric of history, so as to transform all things into saving grace in time, and with infinite and inalterable patience bring to realization the final coming of the kingdom of God.

Firm in this faith, we can also add that it is the support of the Holy Spirit which gives to the Church her ability to extend her boundaries and to live with enthusiasm her missionary adventure. Likewise to be ascribed to the presence of the Holy Spirit is the fact that she is not hesitant about participating in the discussion of serious and valid questions, offering her statements in an unequivocal, serious and decisive manner. And how, then, explain the confidence, the optimism, the condescension and historic patience of this Spouse of Christ except through the richness of the Holy Spirit of Love who, unseen, vitalizes all the ecclesial texture? It is the power of the Spirit which makes the Church the true mother of all by bringing into being a "civilization of love." "Only when illuminated and animated by the Spirit can the Church offer herself to the world as a visible image and as the hope of that which humanity is called to become" (Cardinal Suenens).

It is good to complete this picture of light and victory by giving thought to the normalizing and providential action patiently exercised by the Holy Spirit in the Church, immersed as she is in the shadows and sins which condition the vitality of the Mystical Body of Christ. The Church is made up of human beings and is always surrounded by what is contingent and precarious; therefore she is continually running the risk of being contaminated by the world, as she experiences daily her own ethical fragility, finding herself not infrequently mediocre, sinful, and sometimes far from the evangelical ideal. But this very fact is first of all an assurance that the Church is closely bound to the weaknesses and insufficiencies of humanity; it is further and quite importantly a providential condition for the triumph of divine patience. It is actually this divine Spirit who calls us to perfection when and as He wills, accomplishing His victories precisely through our continual weakness as He acts in our souls with eternal patience and with absolute liberty.

Secondly, it is this very humanness of the Church which makes her understanding and renders her expert in dealing with sinful and mortal humanity. Some of us, in face of the evil—real or imaginary—of other brethren, want to have recourse to violent and punitive action, setting up the policy of "either-or," and wishing to excommunicate the weaker members. But the Church is a realm of patience and of hope; she tolerates the presence of sinners and even the wicked because her office, like that of the Savior, is to restore and transform rather than to strike down and destroy. And it is the very limitation of her members, who are placed in responsible positions which urges her to adopt and set as a norm this method of infinite indulgence as she reflects on all the miseries of the world.

We must not forget, finally, that in the face of a perennial admixture of good and evil, of virtue and vice, it is God Himself who is desirous of manifesting His patience and longsuffering. He leaves to each person the maturing of his own conversion, up to the moment when the weeds will be separated from the good wheat at the end of time. And if this is God's way, the method of the Holy Spirit, what right have we to become irritated at human limitations, including those of Christians?

We adore You, O Holy Spirit!
You are the breath and the ardor through
    which the Word of God comes to us.
Only through Your action do we arrive at the
    knowledge that Jesus Christ is living,
and at the happiness of following Him as
    our way of salvation.

O Holy Spirit,
You are promise and security, You are silence
    and grace.
You are enthusiasm and effective, irresistible
    strength.
We pray You, awaken us to life as You did in
    the beginning of time,
creating and re-creating man.
Place within us Your life-giving energy
so that we may give testimony to Your
    exalted presence in the Church.

O eternal Love of God,
make us sharers in Your light and Your fire of
    love,
and give us great patience and mercy
so that we may be able to support all with
    love and hope,
today and always,
to the fullness of glory in eternity.

The Holy Spirit and His Hidden Presence in History

Not only is the Holy Spirit the prime actor in every conversion within each soul and within the Church; He is also the patient and victorious designer of the events of history. History is more than a purely human record of man's past; it is a wonderful epiphany of the divine plan of salvation unfolding under the direction and power of God "in whom we live and move and have our being" (cf. Acts 17:28).

It is told that the ancients of Israel insisted on having a king, as the other nations had. The Lord, however, was of a different mind, on two scores: first, if a king were placed over Israel it would indicate a betrayal of the pact of love between the Chosen People and their God; and, secondly, a king would requisition from the people their cattle, the women, and the fruits of the field in order to adorn his palace and enrich his courtiers. But the people, heedless of the words of the prophet Samuel, renewed their insistence on a king. And so it took place. Hardly had the prophet Samuel consecrated Saul king when the things predicted by the Lord began to happen point by point, and the Israelites had to face one of the saddest and most difficult periods of their history. But the Lord did not withdraw His benevolence. After the failure of Saul's kingdom God placed at his side a vigorous youth, beautiful and fair, filled with enthusiasm, with poetry and promise: his name was David. The Holy Scriptures tell us the story: we read it in the book of Samuel.

> The Lord said to Samuel, "How long will you grieve over Saul, seeing I have rejected him from being king over Israel? Fill your horn with oil, and go; I will send you to Jesse the Bethlehemite, for I have provided for myself a king among his sons.... Take a heifer with you, and say, 'I have come to sacrifice to the Lord.' And invite Jesse to the sacrifice, and I will show you what you shall do; and you shall anoint for me him whom I name to you." Samuel did what the Lord commanded, and came to Bethlehem. The elders of the city came to meet him trembling, and said, "Do you come peaceably?" And he said, "Peaceably; I have come to sacrifice to the Lord; consecrate yourselves, and

come with me to the sacrifice." And he consecrated Jesse and his sons, and invited them to the sacrifice.

Whey they came, he looked on Eliab and thought, "Surely the Lord's anointed is before him." But the Lord said to Samuel, "Do not look on his appearance or on the height of his stature, because I have rejected him; for the Lord sees not as man sees; man looks on the outward appearance, but the Lord looks on the heart." Then Jesse called Abinadab, and made him pass before Samuel. And he said, "Neither has the Lord chosen this one." Then Jesse made Shammah pass by. And he said, "Neither has the Lord chosen this one." And Jesse made seven of his sons pass before Samuel. And Samuel said to Jesse, "The Lord has not chosen these." And Samuel said to Jesse, "Are all your sons here?" And he said, "There remains yet the youngest, but behold, he is keeping the sheep." And Samuel said to Jesse, "Send and fetch him; for we will not sit down till he comes here." And he sent, and brought him in. Now he was ruddy, and had beautiful eyes, and was handsome. And the Lord said, "Arise, anoint him; for this is he." Then Samuel took the horn of oil, and anointed him in the midst of his brothers; and the Spirit of the Lord came mightily upon David from that day forward.

(1 Sm. 16:1, 2-13)*

The course of events in Israel changed so very much through David that the monarchy achieved unhoped-for results for the good of the people and for religion, and remained faithful in the sight of the Lord.

But it is above all in the incarnation that God inserts Himself directly and irreversibly into history. Three times does St. John call the Lord the "alpha et omèga." Just as all the vowels and consonants of our words are letters of the alphabet, so are all events and things a part of the great current of time, influenced by the salvific presence of the Redeemer. We can find great encouragement in the words of the Apostle Paul who tells us that history is the time in which the patience of God is at work, gently but fruitfully, for our sanctification. This seems to be the thought also of Vatican Council II when it affirms that "...the Lord of ages wisely and patiently follows out the plan of His grace on behalf of us sinners" (Decree on Ecumenism, no. 1). It stands as a fact that the Spirit of God in our history is present "from end to end mightily, and ordereth all things sweetly" (Wis. 8:1, Douay). St. Luke, the evangelist of the Church and the disciple of St. Paul, inserts at the very beginning of his Gospel (written about 60 A.D.) two classic hymns, the "Benedictus" and the "Magnificat," giving us glowing promise of the triumph of divine mercy for all people (cf. Lk. 1:46-55; 68-79). The author of the Book of Revelation, in his turn, interpreting contemporary events in the light of the risen Christ, sings of the heavenly Jerusalem as a reality already being accomplished in time through the Church: "Then I saw a new heaven and a new earth; for the first heaven and the first earth had passed away, and the sea was no more. And I saw the holy city, new Jerusalem, coming down out of heaven from God, prepared as a bride adorned for her husband; and I heard a great voice from the throne saying, 'Behold, the dwelling of God is with men. He will dwell with them, and they shall be his people, and God himself will be with them'" (Rv. 21:1-3).*

The activity of the Holy Spirit in the pages of history is not to be interpreted, however, as of a horizontal timeline. Christ, the Conqueror of time and of history, has attained this victory through the paschal mystery, that is, through His death and resurrection. Human history, just because it is human, will always be punctuated with mistakes, with sins, with wickedness and failures; every negative aspect, however, has already been patiently transformed by the salvific power of Christ, and the reality of this transformation will be manifested progressively to the end of time.

Let us now direct our reflections to the perspective of moral obligation. We feel that it will be purposeful to mention here several outstanding points of pastoral significance— that is, what we ought to do or not do in reflecting on our history.

In the first place, let us discard a pessimistic attitude in looking at the things that are or have been. James Monsabré, Dominican orator and writer who died in 1907 at the beginning of our century, exclaimed: "If God were to give me twenty-four hours of His omnipotence, you would see what changes I would make in the world! But, if He were also to give me the gift of His wisdom, then certainly I would be content to leave things as they are." The poet-theologian, Dante Alighieri, seeing with global vision the whole story of the world, of man and of the Church, and noting everywhere the dynamic of an eternal and ineffable forbearance on the part of God, places in the lips of one of his personages—St. Peter Damian—this touching ejaculation: "O Patience, which sustains so much!" (Paradiso, 21, 135)

"We know where history is going, even though we do not know which road it is taking," St. Augustine assures us. History advances with God. Even in this our era, which with good reason could be termed "zero hour," there is hidden somewhere a new spring-time of life. Social disorder does not immobilize the omnipotent hand of God.

Yes, history is made by men, but there is a power within it that goes beyond men; it is guided by God who with patience directs it toward the goals of our justification and our hope (cf. Rom. 3:36; 2 Pt. 3:15), up to the very time when "all peoples will come and adore the Lord, all will glorify his name, for he alone is great, he alone performs marvels" (cf. Ps. 86:9-10).

Another necessary lesson for us, therefore, is to learn how to wait. Knowing how to wait is knowing how to be in resonance with the thoughts and the ways of God, who continually urges us to turn to Him anew. The grain waits to mature in the distended and golden spikes, the tree waits to burst forth in blossoms and fruits, the whole of creation waits for the manifestation of the children of God. The Church waits as she passes through the streets of the world to sow the seeds of the Gospel, and God Himself waits, God who time after time is born again and grows in every single person of good will. History is one great waiting-time, one great advent to the very end of time, when the fruit-filled Church will sing with jubilant hosannas: "Come, Lord Jesus!" (Rv. 22:20)

Nothing further remains to us then but to praise and thank God for this His gift of infinite patience and mercy, and to sing with the psalmist:

Let the heavens be glad, and let the earth
    rejoice;
Then shall all the trees of the wood sing for
    joy
    before the Lord, for he comes,
    for he comes to judge the earth (Ps. 96).*

All the ends of the earth have seen
    the victory of our God.
Make a joyful noise to the Lord, all the
    earth;
    break forth into joyous song and sing
    praises! (Ps. 98)*

I will give thanks to you, O Lord, among
    the peoples,
    I will sing praises to you among the
    nations.
For your steadfast love is great above
    the heavens,
    your faithfulness reaches to the clouds
    (Ps. 108).*

All your works shall give thanks to you,
    O Lord,
    and all your saints shall bless you!
They shall speak of the glory of your
    kingdom,
    and tell of your power (Ps. 145).*

Let them praise the name of the Lord,
    for his name alone is exalted;
    his glory is above earth and heaven...
    for the people of Israel who are near to
    him (Ps. 148).*

The Pardon of God: Focal Point of Divine Patience

As long as world has been world, history has continually been polluted by the triad of sins pointed out by the Apostle St. John: pride, avarice, and concupiscence (cf. 1 Jn. 2:16), in other words, by the three wild beasts of Dante's poem: the lion, the wolf, and the leopard (cf. Inf. 1:45-49, 32). So it was at the time of Cain and Abel when 25 percent of humanity was guilty of homicide; so it was at the time of Noah when the flood came to punish mankind for the corruption man had brought upon the earth; so it was at the tower of Babel when men were so proud they despised God Himself. Unfortunately, so it is even today in our world darkened by wars, by personal and group egoism, by violence of every kind, and by the solicitations of pornography.

This is man! We believe ourselves self-sufficient, we set up our persons upon an altar, we break what we find, we soil what we touch, we bellow big words to hide the poverty of our concepts, we sell ourselves to the highest bidder, we disdain the person who differs from us, we try to crush our weaker brother and to belittle the stronger one, we seek in every way to have more, to appear greater, without taking care to be great in soul, to become better, to ennoble ourselves.

Who can ever liberate us from this "law of sin" (Rom. 7:27)? Certainly we cannot save ourselves from ourselves. A sinful, frustrated person is like a pendulum whose main spring is broken: it cannot repair itself. Even doctors, when they are ill, let themselves be cured by others. Further, it is only common sense to take a broken object to the one who knows all its working parts. One does not take a watch to a carpenter to be fixed, neither do we invite a professional theologian to repair the motor of our car. Applying this truism at the level of religious experience, it is only right and proper to maintain that God alone, our Creator and Redeemer, can cure us radically, in our whole being. This cure is effected through the divine pardon bestowed upon us by the Lord, whose essence is mercy and whose joy is to renew all things on the face of the earth.

Pardon is love in its highest and noblest expression, as is suggested by the etymology of the Latin word *per donum*. Perfect pardon can come solely from one who is utterly innocent, that is, from one who cannot harm and therefore cannot have need of the pardon of others. Only in God is this possible. Each one of us has need of being pardoned by our neighbor for something or other: often enough our pardon is rather justice. Only the Lord, by nature, can gratuitously pardon.

Still more. When God pardons us He produces innocence in our soul: it is like a new creation, a real rehabilitation, an ontological and functional transfiguration of all our essence as children of God. Under this aspect, too, only the Lord can truly pardon.

And it is precisely in pardoning that God can manifest and radiate His power as a loving and patient Father—all His mercy, as the liturgy of the Church repeats so often. An unhandy, inefficient person throws away the broken things; but the efficient and capable artist is delighted to show his technical skills in repairing what is broken and restoring faded beauty, in making functional again something that has been reduced to worthlessness. This is God's way, the way of healing what has been wounded, of curing what is sick, of restoring life where there is death, and of reviving hope where despair and failure have prevailed. In turning over the pages of the Sacred Scripture and meditating on the words of the prophets we come to the awareness that what God most desires is to forgive sin, and it is especially in His forgiving love that He manifests His patience, His power of mercy. It is the Lord to whom the king sings in his canticle: "You have thrust all my sins behind your back" (Is. 38:17); with His pardon He delights in showing mercy, and "treads down to the bottom of the sea all our faults" (Mi. 7:18-19); He makes our sins disappear forever. The Lord tells us in the words of Isaiah: "Though your sins are like scarlet, they shall be as white as snow" (Is. 1:18).

Laszio Mecs, a Hungarian poet, sings:

In the heart of God every man finds his place:
the more sullied he is, the purer the water
    glistens.
In this water the Magyaro and the Buddhist
    become clean,
the Christian and the idolater, the killer
    and the traitor,
the sadist, the leper....
Brother! Through the love of God
we are white as snow and the lotus blossom!

But it is in Christ Jesus that divine pardon is most ardent, filled with human affection and incomparable patience. The Incarnation is God made tenderness for our sins. It is significant that this is Christ's habitual attitude: He speaks to the crowds, feeds the hungry, and cures the sick who are brought to Him; but when there is occasion for granting pardon, He accosts the sinners personally, singly, as if to let them taste, each for himself, the delicacy of His patient mercy. So it was for the adulteress, for the Samaritan, for the sinful woman, for Peter, for Levi (the Apostle Matthew), for Paul, for others. But there is another precious note in the pardon He grants: though admitting the dark reality of sin, Christ does not humiliate, He does not give a stinging reproof; rather He finds joy in pardoning, in healing, in restoring, in making His creatures new again, in making them apostles. There is a great difference between reproof and pardon. The one magnifies the fault, the other disregards it. Reproof humiliates the person who has made a mistake; pardon invites him to return to his former status. Reproof is often a sign of pride in the person who gives it; pardon, on the contrary, is empathy and a sharing in the sorrow of the one who has done wrong. Reproof is addressed to the past when the sin was committed; pardon is a message of hope and optimism for a better future. Concretely, reproof is the revenge of man, while pardon is the way of the love and patience of God.

But it is Calvary that most forcefully offers a singular and indicative grasp of the concept of Christ as Savior and Redeemer. According to the Hebraic pattern of thought, juridical in its nature, a testimony can be accepted as true if there are two witnesses (cf. also Jn. 8:17). Well then: Christ was crucified between two thieves as if to convince men once and for always that He was poured out in sacrifice to merit the pardon and Redemption of all the sinners of the world. And as His death took place outside the Holy City, it gave assurance of salvaging the outcasts, the rejected, the abandoned, all the workers of iniquity, offering as the price of pardon His own blood. St. Augustine, echoing St. Paul whom he studied assiduously, speaks eloquently in the tenth book of his masterpiece, *The Confessions*, about the mercy of the Savior. He points out that Christ is the Mediator between the Father and the human race when as invincible justice He takes a place among sinners in order to gain the victory over sin. He in whom are hidden the treasures of wisdom and knowledge has willed to give His blood for us. And then in a mystical thrust, this sainted son of St. Monica addresses the Lord with the ardent prayer:

See, Lord, I cast my care upon Thee,
    that I may live

and consider the wonderful things
    of Thy law.
Thou knowest my lack of skill and my
    infirmity,
oh, teach me and heal me!
That dear Son of Thine, in whom are hid
all the treasures of wisdom and knowledge,
hath redeemed me with His blood...
How didst Thou love us, O good Father!

Ezekiel, priest and prophet, foresaw the Messiah as the Good Shepherd *par excellence*, and under that image he described Him:

As a shepherd seeks out his flock when some of his sheep have been scattered abroad, so will I seek out my sheep; and I will rescue them from all places where they have been scattered on a day of clouds and thick darkness.... I will bring them into their own land; and I will feed them on the mountains of Israel, by the fountains, and in all the inhabited places of the country. I will feed them with good pasture, and upon the mountain heights of Israel shall be their pasture; there they shall lie down in good grazing land, and on fat pasture they shall feed on the mountains of Israel. I myself will be the shepherd of my sheep, and I will make them lie down.... I will seek the lost, and I will bring back the strayed, and I will bind up the crippled, and I will strengthen the weak, and the fat and the strong I will watch over; I will feed them in justice (Ez. 34: *passim* 5-23).*

This Good Shepherd, St. John the Evangelist informs us further, knows each one of His sheep, He goes out to aid the wounded one, and at the cost of His own life He defends the flock from the wolf. The Apostle of Love continues by telling us that Jesus, the peerless Good Shepherd of our souls, draws us to Himself to let us repose on His heart, and He carries us on His shoulders as a mother takes a child into her arms (cf. Jn. 10:1-18).

It seems quite fitting in this context to reflect on an important episode related in the Gospel, the story of the public sinner who entered the house of Simon the Pharisee to ask pardon of Jesus for her sins. The "evangelist of God's tenderness"—St. Luke—in a first-class scenario relates the happening and offers with it a number of wholesome gems for the enrichment of the spirit:

> One of the Pharisees asked him to eat with him and he went into the Pharisee's house, and sat at table. And behold, a woman of the city, who was a sinner, when she learned that he was sitting at table in the Pharisee's house, brought an alabaster flask of ointment, and standing behind him at his feet, weeping, she began to wet his feet with her tears, and wiped them with the hair of her head, and kissed his feet, and anointed

them with the ointment. Now when the Pharisee who had invited him saw it, he said to himself, "If this man were a prophet, he would have known who and what sort of woman this is who is touching him, for she is a sinner." And Jesus answering said to him, 'Simon, I have something to say to you." And he answered, "What is it, Teacher?" "A certain creditor had two debtors; one owed five hundred denarii, and the other fifty. When they could not pay, he forgave them both. Now which of them will love him more?" Simon answered, "The one, I suppose, to whom he forgave more." And he said to him, "You have judged rightly." Then turning toward the woman he said to Simon, "Do you see this woman? I entered your house, you gave me no water for my feet, but she has wet my feet with her tears and wiped them with her hair. You gave me no kiss, but from the time I came in she has not ceased to kiss my feet. You did not anoint my head with oil, but she has anointed my feet with ointment. Therefore I tell you, her sins, which are many, are forgiven, for she loved much; but he who is forgiven little, loves little." And he said to her, "Your sins are forgiven." Then those who were at table with him began to say among themselves, "Who is this, who even forgives sins?" And he said to the woman, "Your faith has saved you; go in peace."   (Lk. 7:36-50)*

It is to be noted in the first place that this sinner is not the Magdalene, nor is it Mary the sister of Lazarus. It is an anonymous sinner, one among the many who lived there at the time. The evangelist does not concern himself about giving her a name, either out of a certain sense of delicacy in regard to this particular woman, or else in the sense that this sinner could stand as a symbol and hope for all the sinners of the world.

As a point in catechesis it is to be noted, secondly, that the woman has a vivid awareness of the gravity of sin. Certainly she must have had other sorrows, but she pours out her tears over the one misfortune of life, sin. And then to annul totally her guilt, she thinks and acts audaciously, overcoming every obstacle to approach Jesus, subjecting herself to the darts of the malicious judgments of the banquet guests and reducing to nought the gratifying sense of pleasurable feasting.

The realization of her sin does not envelope her in a feeling of despair, however, for she knows that there is a Savior. It is not improbable that this sinner had encountered the Master earlier and had listened to His teaching, all keyed to mercy. Now in this meeting with the Messiah in Simon's house, it was her determination to enter into the very heart of God, to be immersed in His infinite love. The Danish poet-philosopher Sören Kierkegaard who died in 1855 at only 43 years of age, tells us in his writings that through the "happy spiral of divine love" our sin, absorbed by the goodness of Christ, becomes the very foundation of the fullness of love between the Redeemer and the pardoned soul.

In effect, while purely legal justice in itself represses the sinner and gouges out a dizzying abyss between the judge and the culprit, love on the contrary accepts the sinner and places him in the sure way of friendship and communion.

St. Luke, the evangelist who was also a physician, is likewise preoccupied in making evident the pedagogy and delicacy of the method of Christ, who far from scolding the sinner, as the Pharisee and his company would have done, holds her up as one who has done a generous act of kindness. Perhaps for us, too, this method used by Jesus will be an incentive to distinguish between the error and the erring. St. Augustine, master of clear and luminous phrasing, tells us that "it is necessary to love the man but not his error; man is made by God, error is made by man; it is necessary to love the work of God and not that of man." In other words: we must condemn the sin but always respect the sinner.

Undoubtedly the most touching aspect of this episode is the totality of the love of the pardoned woman. The eyes from which her tears flow, the hair with which she dries the Lord's feet, the lips with which she kisses, the perfume she pours out upon His feet, everything which formerly could have been the means of seduction and of pleasure is transformed into a hymn of love and gratitude. And even though the woman says not a word from the beginning to the end, her whole being expresses her grateful love. Any word would have been a futile and inadequate vehicle to convey the totality of her womanly sentiments, now fully reclaimed in the strength of divine love.

Thus this anonymous sinner has become unforgettable in history, while all her sins have been forgotten. Without saying any word at all she has succeeded in filling our hearts with hope and joy, because she has shown and demonstrated to us that Jesus is the "true Lamb who takes away the sins of the world."

Several pertinent reflections on the infinite mercy of God will serve to invigorate our Christian vocation with new zeal and enthusiasm.

First place must be given to the measure of our trust in the goodness and patience of God, a confidence which must be practical and all-embracing. A prayer from the Lenten liturgy expresses well our sentiment of trust in divine mercy: "Accept, O gracious Lord, the prayers and tears your people pour out at this holy time. You who see and know the secrets of the heart, grant to penitents the grace of pardon. Our sin is great, but your love is greater. Cancel our debts for the glory of your name!"

St. Cyril of Jerusalem, Doctor of the Church (d. 386), comments thus on the mercy of God: "If all our sins were placed one upon the other they would never overpower the indulgence of God, just as all sorts of wounds never surpass the arts and skills of the physician." Even if our sins were as numerous as the drops of water in the sea, as immense as a mountain, the infinite mercy of God would always be greater and more abundant as St. John the Apostle assures us (cf. 1 Jn. 3:5-20). Dante Alighieri places upon the lips of Manfred of Swabia, son of Frederick II and nephew of Constansa, these celebrated words:

> Should it happen that I run my sword
> through a person

and leave him with two mortal wounds,
    then weeping
I would hasten to Him who willingly
    pardons.

My sins have been horrible,
but infinite goodness has such a wide
    embrace
that it welcomes whatever enters within it.
                (Purg. III, 123)

A second point for reflection is the truth that even if we were to refuse the divine offer of pardon, God would continue to wait for us and would have confidence in us to the very last breath of our life. This is confirmed in the following authentic account: Vladimir Lenin, a victim of thrombosis, lay very close to death. One day quite unexpectedly he questioned his attending physician: "Are you a believer?" "Yes," answered the doctor. Then Lenin asked him if he knew of any ecclesiastical person of Moscow who was not engaged in politics. The name of Bishop Trifon was given, and Lenin asked to make his acquaintance. The next day the doctor brought Bishop Trifon to the founder of bolshevism. Lenin and the Bishop remained together for two hours.... Another day, it is told, Lenin begged an elderly woman who was assisting him: "Nonnina (Little Granny), pray to the Lord for me! Don't tell anyone but pray!" The following day the little old lady was ordered never again to enter the house of the revolutionary. If this episode is true—and no one can affirm the contrary—we have the right to presume that God's pardon triumphed in the end.

It is known that Dante places on the lips of a demon a mocking lament against an angel of God, who snatches from him a notorious sinner because of a little act of penance he offered just before his death. "O you of heaven," cried the demon, "why do you deprive me? You take him away from me and give him heaven because of a little tear!" (cf. Purg. V, 104-105)

To believe in the love of God is to believe above all in His pardon. St. Augustine almost soars in his passionate exposition of God's loving mercy as quoted by Giulio Domenico Giovanni: "Mortals! Your God does not desire the death of the one who offends Him, He wills that the sinner return to Him and live. Infinite goodness has set His throne upon earth for the advantage of all, and He invites all to find shelter in its shade.... Divine mercy pardons the sinner who has recourse to it, and pays the debts contracted against the sovereign Majesty and His justice. On whatever day the impious person casts himself into the arms of mercy, she will receive him, protect him, save him. Ah, let each one fear only to go away from his God and not return to His love!

Do not imitate me—Augustine—who went far away from His love; but if anyone has imitated me in this my fall, let him now run to the feet of his God and weep for all his evil deeds, and God will be for him a tender and affectionate Father to his last breath" (cf. *Le Veglie*, ed. Grazzini-Maccioni, 1962, p. 251).

Our third moral reflection: For the Christian, the juncture of the two antithetical extremes—the pole of the pardon of God and the pole of the sin of man—happens principally by means of the Church. In His creation, the Lord makes us cognizant of His existence; through the reflection of Himself in nature He tells us that He is. In Sacred Scripture He expressly tells us that He is. Through His Church, however, He wills to let us know what He desires to do for us: to free us from sin and from domination of earthly attachments. As we contemplate this thought, let us not forget that the first gift the risen Christ gave to His Church was the Holy Spirit, for the forgiveness of sins (cf. Jn. 20:22-23). As we know, this forgiveness is imparted by Holy Church in the Sacrament of Penance, in which the priest is the minister of the patience of God (cf. Vat. II, Priestly Life and Ministry, 5; 13).

Penance is the sacrament of the most intimate friendship between the creature and the Creator. It is also a sacrament of the worship and praise of God, for the penitent praises the highest attributes of the Lord, His patience and mercy, His power, His indulgence and condescension—the magnanimity of God from whom alone can come the pardon granted, and the security and joy of renewed grace.

> Recall, then, all that you have been in thoughts, words and works...show yourself to God, call upon Him, weep. No wound must be concealed, no scar withheld from the caress of His fatherly goodness.... Knock loudly at the door of joy; knock, pray, and weep; there is your home. The father is there and is waiting for you. Here is the door which opens upon a sea of light; sweet mercy opens the door to welcome you. And the weight of human misery melts away like ice in the sun, life is renewed like the burgeoning seed on an April morning, and the colloquy between you and the Lord interweaves like sorrow and joy, like sun and rain. Everything takes on the transparency of dawn, freshened with showers and dried by sunshine.
>
> (Carl Cremona: *Sins of the Curate*, p. 213)

Our fourth reflection is the joy effected by divine pardon, joy for the Lord and joy for the pardoned penitent. In a fourteenth-century antiphonary in the Cathedral of Siena is an exquisite miniature representing the Sacrament of Reconciliation. A priest is shown absolving a kneeling man, while in the sky above, jubilant angels play harps and sing hymns. In his novel, *The Idiot*, Fedoro Dostoevski briskly sketches a delicate scene: As the idiot observes a mother tracing the Sign of the Cross on the breast of her tiny infant he asks: "Why are you doing that?" "Because my little one has smiled, and when a mother sees her baby smiling for the first time she rejoices as God does when He sees a penitent sinner." So true! A converted heart fills paradise with joy!

So too does the recipient of divine pardon exult with inexpressible joy. Benigno Bossuet, the prince of the sacred orators of the seventeenth century, writes: "Among all those who weep, the first and the only ones to be consoled are those who weep for their sins. Sorrow in itself is not a remedy for evil; sometimes it rather augments a suffering. Only the tears poured out for our sins are sweet tears, full of hope, bright with joy." The French convert, Adolf Retté, who died in 1930, described his sentiments upon his return to his Father's house: "Hardly had I received pardon and entered again into friendship with God when it seemed to me that a hundred Alleluias were singing in my heart!"

Our last reflection might well be our resolution. It is said that men are pure only in the cradle, as rivers are pure only at their source. But our greatest glory is not that we never fall, but that we always rise again with confidence. We all remain more or less wounded by our human condition, but nothing is lost if we come out humble and purified. Innocence is beautiful and wonderful, but repentance and spiritual renovation are a reflection of the beauty of God and a sign of His divine power.

What is the mercy of God? The etymology of the Latin term *misericordia* informs us that it is the heart of God touching and transfiguring our misery. If a photograph of someone we love should happen to fall to the floor, see how we instinctively pick it up and kiss it. Thus does our heavenly Father treat us when we fall or die through sin. God is an abyss, an abyss of love. "Paternal abyss," Origen calls Him. The psalmist says: "Abyss calls to abyss," that is, as the German mystic Silesius comments, "The abyss of my spirit ceases not to cry out to the abyss of God, whose love is all His richness and whose mercy is all His wisdom."

There is no doubt that the normal person, in the face of the bitter experience of his sin and his "little nothingness," feels the need of having Someone who can reclaim him, who can save him. This is our yearning and our hope.

To be more or less among the prodigal sons is the lot of all, but we may not remain far from the Father! To return home even if we are ragged, soiled, empty-handed is certainly an undertaking that demands our good will, but it is always better than remaining far from home with a broken heart.

To return to the Father and ask to take the last place can be humbling to our egoism, but when we reflect that God is waiting for us, fear becomes confidence and humiliation is transformed into victory and rejoicing.

Mother Speranza of the Congregation of Merciful Love exhorts us in these words: "If anyone of you has had the misfortune of offending the Lord by sin, never hesitate in the least, not even for a moment, to hasten to Him and ask to be pardoned and to be received again in His fatherly embrace. God Himself is waiting for this with yearning, with deep affection.... And you can testify that merciful Love has always attracted us with infinite sweetness. You will be surprised at seeing His love and His goodness when you had imagined Him displeased, with a sword in His hand ready to punish."

Lord, every time I sin You place within me a
desire for pardon.
You give me strength to start out once again
on my journey toward You, O Father rich in
mercy!
Even when I am a sinner, I remain always
Your child,
and therefore You expect and desire of me
that I seek Your goodness and joy,
without losing my peace in lamenting my sin.
Lord, I would like to tell You one by one all
my misdeeds,
announce with a loud voice all my vileness,
but You, instead, are more concerned about
preparing a feast
for this Your son, who, believing in Your
love,
has returned to the family.
Lord, after every tempest, help me return to
You,
to the Church, spiritual home of men,
to let my spirit blossom with true liberty and
peace,
and be able to taste the ineffable joy of Your
fatherly pardon.

Why God
Is Patient with Us

The first explanation of the patience of God toward us is the *absolute gratuity of His love for us.* St. Augustine distinguishes three kinds of love: to love in order to be loved, to love simply to love, and to love in order to give oneself freely to another. The goodness of God belongs to this third kind of love. Love is not just one of God's attributes, it is His essence. God loves totally, unconditionally, universally. He loves everywhere and everyone. For Him, to give Himself is to be Himself, to pour Himself out is to live and act according to His nature. The radiant newness of the Christian message, repeated for us at least twice by St. John the Apostle, is this: "God is love" (Jn. 4:8, 16). The Servant of God, Louisa Margareta de la Touche, said of Him: "If He were to cease to love, He would cease to be God."

God's love for us is absolute, and what is absolute is not relative to anyone. What is absolute is free from any conditioning, from any recall, any response or compensation. We, unfortunately, when we say we love someone, often condition the offering of our love with "ifs" and "buts"; but with absolute liberty the Lord loves without being blocked by human response.

We might complete this explanation by recalling that the Lord, because He is God—the simple Being *par excellence*—has no need of manifesting His love in giving and receiving as if any qualitative enrichment were possible to His being. It is no wonder then that the Lord has willed to be for us Father, Brother, Friend. "No one is equal to Him as father, no one can match His goodness," Tertullian stated. And Isaiah reminds us that He is the incomparable mother (cf. Is. 49:15). No one measures up to Him in patience.

Who are Christians? They are the beloved, the favored of God, they are the ones called by Jesus Christ and held in His immense love, they are the ones enriched and filled in abundance with the peace, the charity and the mercy of the Lord.

We must make a second reflection, complementary to the first, on the *fidelity* of God, the cause and manner of all His infinite patience toward us. According to biblical concepts the divine fidelity, called *emet* in Hebrew, is the coronation of mercy, and it signifies an uninterrupted and patient offering of benevolence on the part of the Lord toward the human creature in all the countless and most varied situations in which he finds himself. Like stars in the heavens, the *emet* of the Lord shines in the pages of the Bible, and the word fidelity is a recurring refrain of the salvific message.

God is always faithful in His mercy. Certainly He does not deprive man of his existential and historical drama, but He lives it with him. For all time the Lord has made His dwelling among men to remain always with us (cf. Ex. 29:45; 33:7-11). As the waters of the sea wash against the rock, so are we ceaselessly followed and accompanied by the loving fidelity of God. For the thousands and thousands of generations since time began, this merciful love has been bestowed on man in kindness and faithfulness (cf. Ex. 34:6-7). "Yahweh is merciful and tenderhearted; he never forgets the covenant he has made with us" (Ps. 111:4-5).

On God's part, therefore, there will never be a diminishing of love, for He is faithful. "If we are faithless, he remains faithful—for he cannot deny himself" (2 Tm. 2:13).* "For the mountains may depart and the hills be removed, but my steadfast love shall not depart from you, and my covenant of peace shall not be removed..." (Is. 54:10),* because "I have

loved you with an everlasting love" (Jer. 31:3).*
The holy fidelity of God persists in following
us despite all our infidelities. Just as a light
does not cease to shine upon a closed door, so
does celestial mercy never cease to accompany
us in order to save us (cf. Bar. 5:9; Ps. 69:14).
Even if we should lose confidence in the Lord,
He will continue to have confidence and hope
in us. And only if the Lord would cease to be
infinitely good and merciful, and we should
become totally and infinitely evil and un-
faithful—both metaphysical impossibilities—
until such a time there will always be for us
the possibility of salvation and of rebirth.

It is this very "divine high fidelity," all
fragrant with indulgence and compassion,
which gives wings and optimism to our spiritual and social activities, and prompts us to
sing to the Lord—as did the ancient Israelites—a canticle of thanksgiving so spontane-
ous, hearty and vigorous that it pierces the
starry vaults of heaven (Ps. 3:6; 40:11-12;
69:14; 98:3; etc.).

Just as love includes this quality of fidelity, so must this virtue, in turn, have as its
companion in activity the noble grace of
condescension.

What is the history of salvation if not a
perennial and providential *condescension of God*

toward humanity? What is the history of the covenant if not the surpassing adaptation of divine power to all the vicissitudes and customs of a people, the Hebrews? After the manifestation of God on Sinai and the renovation of the covenant already made with the head of the tribe, Abraham, God wished to be still closer to His people to be their light, guide, and strength. From that time on, the manifest presence of God among men became more fixed: "I shall dwell in the midst of the sons of Israel," says the Lord, "and I shall be their God" (Ex. 29:45). The place and symbol of this new intimacy between heaven and earth is a movable sanctuary, the so-called "Tabernacle" or "Tent of Meeting" which the people of God carried with them in their wanderings through the desert. The book of Exodus tells us: "Moses used to take the tent and pitch it outside the camp.... And every one who sought the Lord would go out to the tent of meeting, which was outside the camp. Whenever Moses went out to the tent, all the people rose up, and every man stood at his tent door, and looked after Moses, until he had gone into the tent. When Moses entered the tent, the pillar of cloud would descend and stand at the door of the tent, and the Lord would speak with Moses. And when all the people saw the pillar of cloud standing at the door of the tent, all the people would rise up and worship, every man at his tent door. Thus the Lord used to speak to Moses face to face, as a man speaks to his friend. Moses turned again into the camp..." (33:7-11).* Undoubtedly the seat of the glory of the Most High remained the most touching sign of the familiarity of God. We know that by day this cloud moved in front of the people to guide them securely (if it had been right in the midst of the Israelites it would have produced error and confusion), while at night it became permeated with fire, giving light and heat for the comfort of the pilgrims (cf. Ex. 40:38).

Divine condescension is clearly evident in the very language the Lord uses to dialogue with His elect. Here our teacher is St. John Chrysostom, perhaps the only Doctor of the Church who has investigated and written abundantly on the Bible as the classic exposition of *sin-katábasis*, the Greek term for divine condescension. This great orator and patriarch of Constantinople, who died on September 14, 407, affirms that the Lord gives the greatest mark of condescension to His Chosen People by respecting their way of speaking, and by assuming for Himself the poverty of verbal expression with the coloring of the mentality of this Oriental people. God is not preoccupied about speaking in consonance with His dignity; He dialogues only for the benefit of His listeners. Even when the Lord makes use of persons—the prophets—to transmit His message of love and fidelity, He does not annihilate the personality and the verbal mannerisms of these persons; rather, He adapts Himself to them, to their style and their humors, in order to be friendly and accommodating with Israel. And all this—comments and concludes St. John Chrysostom—is the most radiant epiphany of the patience of God.

> A classic example of humble condescension on the part of God in dialogue with His people is to be found in chapter 24 (vv. 1-13) of the book of Joshua, in which the Lord, through Joshua, recalls and enumerates all the works done for the benefit of the people of Israel, as if to call forth gratitude and collaboration. The prophet Isaiah describes God as one who summons His people to Himself to "talk this over," face to face (cf. Is. 1:18).

It will serve us well to reflect for a moment upon our actual *human weakness* and *fragility*, a condition which certainly is one of the reasons for God's infinite patience toward us. A Spanish legend tells us: When God was preparing to create man, the angels—pure intelligences—assembled to discuss how they could dissuade the Lord from this enterprise of creating a being with a twofold ontology.

Such a being would necessarily be complicated in his actions, complex in his ideas and sentiments. Then the most illustrious angel of paradise, the moderator of this angelic conference, humbly and timidly presented himself before the Supreme Lord to report in confidence all that had been discussed in the angelic assembly. "Father omnipotent, supreme Creator of all things and of every creature," began the celestial spokesperson, "You are planning to create a being which is too complicated. He would be composed of soul and body, of matter and spirit, of flesh and feeling, of intelligence and passion, of love and hate, of high hopes and dense despair; on the one hand he would be as great as we, but on the other, he would be made up of weaknesses and miseries like the animals. Do not create him like this, Lord of all things, for if he is created with these complications, it will be just this very being who will give You much trouble and commit many sins."

The Lord—continues the legend—listened attentively to the speech and the opinions the angels had given, and then responded solemnly and decisively: "All these things you say, my angelic messenger, are true, but if it is my will that man be made in this fashion, why do you not accept my design, why do you not presume that in this problem there may be other reasons that you do not know?" And the angel, having completed his mission, returned to his own without having gained any concession from God.

Interpreting the legend on a biblical note, we find no difficulty in admitting that man is, by constitution, truly a mixture of good and evil. God knows it, and for this reason He is patient with us. Isaiah writes: "All the nations are as nothing before him, they are accounted by him as less than nothing and emptiness" (40:17).* And the psalmist sings: "As the father has compassion on his children, so is God patient with us; he remembers that we are dust.... Many times the Lord has moderated his wrath and subdued his anger, remembering that we are flesh and like a wind which comes and goes" (cf. Ps. 103:13-14; 78:38-39). Sirach reminds us that God is very patient with us because He knows we are a very little thing; we are like drops of water and grains of sand (cf. Sir. 18:9-11).

It has been said justly that the creation of man was a "divine risk," but we can be sure that God will always love us because we are His creatures, because we are so weak, small and fragile. He will follow us always and everywhere with His patience, despite or even because of our natural insufficiency, for He is mercy. St. Augustine, in one of his frequent mystical flights in praise of the

Creator, expresses it like this: "Our human nature is the work of Him who has produced the stars and the firmament. God is Father of all. Every person, whether of nobility or of low social class, is dear to Him. Before Him all men are equal, like the green grasses of a deep valley seen from the heights of a mountain. The Lord loves and follows all: the king and the subject, the famous and the unknown. For the Lord, the greatness of every man is his being a man: no other title surpasses this one."

We can complete this summary by stating, as a final thought, that *God is patient because He is humble*. It is not paradoxical to affirm in human terms that humility is a quality of the divine essence and is the most radical aspect of the oblative love of God. In truth, only one who is humble can give himself without making a burden of his gift, without placing himself at the center of his donation, without demanding recompense. If love is not humble, it is void of its essential content. If one should say, "I love you because I am of more account than you," this person has no right to say, "I love you." For this reason God, the plenitude of love, often manifests His goodness toward us with the divine music of silence (cf. 1 Kgs. 19:11-13). For this reason there is in the depths of divinity the power of making nothing of self, or, to express it as St. Paul does, the power of *kenosis*. (Cf. the famous second chapter of his letter to the Philippians.) God emptied Himself so that He could be easily known. Simone Weil says, "He could create, but only by concealing Himself; otherwise there would have been Himself alone." If the sun is shining brilliantly in the sky, the depth and infinity of the stars cannot be seen, but at night the starry firmament is revealed in all its splendor and luminous immensity. God has made Himself "the night of humanity, the passion of the cross," precisely to show us the fullness of His essence of love, mercy and patience. Here we find the ineffable majesty of the crucifix.

Let us terminate this first part of our meditation with a thought from the writings of a great medieval thinker: "O Lord, if we are mistaken in believing in Your goodness and patience, then we have been deceived by You Yourself. Actually, what we believe has been confirmed by such great prodigies and signs that only You Yourself could have thought them up!" (Richard of St. Victor, *De Trinitate* 1-2) But we want to believe it all and to entrust ourselves to the patient charity of our God. "We ourselves have known and put our faith in God's love towards ourselves. God is love, and anyone who lives in love lives in God, and God lives in him'' (1 Jn. 4:16).

> O Lord, bring peace into the midst of our turbulence.
> Descend into the depths of our being.
> Disperse our darkness with Your luminous clarity.
> Reclothe our consciences with purity.
> Take possession of them with the sweetness of Your loving presence,
> and grant that always, in composed serenity,
> we await Your coming, O vigilant Friend,
> O protector, O sole dispenser of peace!
>
> (From the Mozarabic Liturgy)

The Response of Man

One of the laws of physics discovered by Isaac Newton says that "for every action there is a corresponding reaction, equal and contrary." This is true also in the spiritual order. In view of the fascinating panorama of the patience of God in our encounter with Him, there follows as counterpart an obligation for us to practice the virtue of patience also, not only in imitation of the Father and in obedience to Him, but also because it is in patience that we can find and possess life (Lk. 21:19). Our life must be a pilgrim way in patience (cf. 1 Cor. 13:7; Ti. 2:2).

What Is Patience?

For the Orientals patience is, in general, the absence of struggle, psychological inertia, renunciation of every desire, even that of being happy. The moral Buddhist, for example, gives this counsel: "Make an island of yourself and be wise," while a maxim of Lao-Tse, Chinese philosopher and ascetic of the fifth century before Christ, spells it out like this: "Empty yourself and you will be filled; possess few things and you will be rich.... One who conquers others has physical strength, but one who renounces himself is truly strong."

Quite similar is the evaluation of the Greeks. The comic poet and dramatist Menander of Athens wrote: "Man, whoever you are, never ask the gods to spare you suffering, but rather ask for resignation." Aristotle calls patience the parent of strength. He, this philosopher from Stagira, claims that the ideal man is the one who flees no evil, he fears nothing and no one, he bears all things lest he be judged as small-souled. It is well known that the ancient epic of Homer celebrated in

Ulysses the man who dared to fight courageously against the misfortunes and calam-
ities decreed by fate. The Stoics of Greece and
of Rome, on the contrary, identified felicity
with ataraxy (tranquillity produced by a
drug), that is to say, with the absolute and
almost impudent lack of emotive reactions to
suffering.

In the Christian sense the word patience
connotes quite different ethical concepts, even
though it has some initial connection with
stoic philosophy.

In the first place, biblical patience is not
a synonym for apathy; neither is it an admixture of anxiety and hope in suffering, a hope
that somehow things will soon change. It is,
rather, a strong and constant activity of
the spirit, marked by humility and by long-
suffering. The Christians of the first ecclesial
communities had to live continually under
persecution; they were convinced that only
through patience, that is, through the acceptance of all the hardship inherent in life and in
history, would they be worthy of the following of Christ. From the first era of the Church,
therefore, patience assumes for the Christian
the value of sharing in the paschal mystery
with anticipation of a future kingdom of glory
and joy (cf. Rom. 5:4-5; 2 Tm. 2:11-12).

But Christian patience is likewise a means
of apostolic service; it is a necessity in the

pastoral work of spreading the Gospel of Christ. The true apostle must have patience. He must know how to wait for the growth of the seed he plants (cf. Mt. 4:26). St. James exhorts: "Be patient, therefore, brethren, until the coming of the Lord. Behold, the farmer waits for the precious fruit of the earth, being patient over it until it receives the early and the late rain. You also be patient " (Jas. 5:7).* The Lord never plants the tree already grown, but He gives the seed for He desires to have man as a patient collaborator in producing abundant fruits.

A third difference between patience understood in a profane sense and that inculcated by the Bible is evident in the behavior of the persons concerned. The pagan who accepts some adverse fortune does so with sadness of heart; while the patient Christian keeps his soul serene and trusting above the wavering of his feelings, for he recognizes in this attitude an evidence of human maturity and spiritual growth. Therefore in its depth the Christian soul remains substantially tranquil, calm, like the quiet in the depths of the ocean even when there are waves tossing on the surface.

If all this is so, then it is not difficult to conclude that Christian patience is an essential element of the virtue of fortitude, of longsuffering, and above all of faith, and of the hope which is not deceptive (cf. Rom. 5:5).

But what unequivocally distinguishes the patience of a Christian from the stoicism of a pagan is the eminently theological character of the former.

After all else has been said, true patience is God, because He alone is absolute and perfect charity. Tertullian in his time stated: "Patience is the nature of God, nongenerated individuality." With the coming of the Son of God upon earth, divine patience is, so to say, enriched with a new dimension, that of *éleos*, that is, mercy, a compassion, touching even the emotional level. God, in Christ, is merciful toward us with a mercy charged with human sentiment that knows the miseries which weigh upon us. A noteworthy presentation of the nature of God's mercy toward us is offered in the encyclical of Pope John Paul II, *Dives in misericordia*, Part IV.

Another substantial difference between stoic and Christian patience extends to the very essence of the Christian virtue. Christian patience is described thus: a gift and strength of God, a torrent of love from which proceeds all our virtue (cf. Ps. 62:6; 36:9). "True patience," comments St. Catherine of Siena, "is the daughter of divine charity." A botanical note handed down to us by Pliny the Elder can help us visualize this idea. The Roman naturalist and historian recounted: "I have seen in Tivoli a tree on which were grafted branches of many kinds of fruits; the tree bore a vast assortment of fruits: cherries hung on one branch, nuts on another, grapes on a third, figs on a fourth, and there were still more—pomegranates, plums, pears, fruits of every kind." St. Francis de Sales made use of this interesting simile in his book *Theotimus*, to demonstrate the influence of divine love in our hearts, the only thing that can make us patient with ourselves, with others and with the world. On this point St. Paul is master *par excellence*. In the first letter this Apostle wrote to the Christians of Corinth, he cast a light upon the dynamic interdependence between the charity of God and the modes of response it can and must have in the heart of man. His manner of developing the theme is incomparable. In the first four verses Paul speaks of charity as the essence of God, and then with an almost unnoticed transition, he sets out to describe all the dynamic and moral facets of this charity, which is operative in all those who have been invaded by God's love. The text reads like this:

> If I speak in the tongues of men and of angels, but have not love, I am a noisy gong or a clanging cymbal. And if I have

prophetic powers, and understand all mysteries and all knowledge, and if I have all faith, so as to remove mountains, but have not love, I am nothing. If I give away all I have, and if I deliver my body to be burned, but have not love, I gain nothing.

Love is patient and kind; love is not jealous or boastful; it is not arrogant or rude. Love does not insist on its own way; it is not irritable or resentful; it does not rejoice at wrong, but rejoices in the right. Love bears all things, believes all things, hopes all things, endures all things. Love never ends...

(1 Cor. 13:1-8).*

A Morning Prayer

Lord, in the silence of this beginning day
I come to ask You for peace, prudence,
    strength and great patience.
Today I wish to look at the world with eyes of
    love;
I want to be understanding, sweet,
    discerning and indulgent.
I desire that beyond the external appearances
    I see You in every person,
and concentrate only on the good in each
    one.
Close my ears to calumny, preserve my
    tongue from speaking evil,

may my spirit be filled with thoughts of
    patience and charity.
Grant that my helpfulness and kindness to all
    whom I meet
may let them perceive Your loving
    omnipresence.
Clothe me with Yourself, Lord, that I may
    radiate Your love all day long,
for the serenity of my brethren.

Necessity of Patience

From the outset we must be convinced that patience is not something secondary in our life; it is an indispensable virtue, necessary for every day and every hour. We have need of patience as the earth has need of rain, of silence, of sunshine, if it is to blossom and mature.

In our era we are dominated by haste and impatience. We are always in a hurry. It seems that everywhere we are losing the ground beneath our feet. More than any preceding generation, ours is inexpressibly nervous: a slight disturbance is sufficient to make us lose our calm. Very few people can claim exemption from a readiness to impatience and discontent. In this our strange society we find in every field of endeavor some individuals who have no regard for a normal growth but rather aim to achieve success immediately. When their achievements do not measure up to their hopes, unpleasant chain reactions hurt them and others. We are extraordinarily incapable of knowing how to wait, how to support life with its laws of growth which are not always appreciated because of our overriding goals.

Our very home can demand a great deal of patience from us. It may happen that one of the children cannot sleep on one night or another and keeps mother and father awake too. Or one of the older ones may have gone out at night without leaving notice, and the other family members are disturbed at the delayed return. Or perhaps some unwelcome guests arrive unannounced, while those we are awaiting cannot arrive on time. Then, too, the telephone rings insistently just at the moment when someone in the family urgently needs our helping hand. Someone knocks at the door—or the doorbell rings—and we go to answer it, sure that the caller is finally the plumber or the electrician we have been awaiting for days; instead we may find ourselves facing a traveling salesman whose face is unfamiliar, even suspicious. And very probably this happens to all people and they need to draw heavily on a supply of patience. There is need for a quiet moment, yet others are chattering noisily, with no regard to an individual's rights, or they insist on entertaining themselves with a noisy television program. Or one has a craving to go out and instead must remain at home because of some unforeseen necessity. Nor is it a rare case that one has an urgent desire to speak one's mind on a certain point, but must be silent in order not to aggravate an already tense family situation. Yes, even the home, which almost by definition should be a haven of refreshment and harmony, can be a place needing mutual forbearance and constant patience.

Perhaps you too have had experiences such as these: you want to make a little business trip into the city and must face unsettling reality. You leave the house in a hurry to go to work, to the office, and you discover that your car will not start. You decide to take the bus, but one has just passed and the next is late in arriving—who knows why? You step into an office to do some business as you have been doing for years, but you have the disappointment of being sent from one window to another and yet another before you finally make any headway. You set out for home, and the heavy traffic in the street takes toll of all the patience you can muster.

And are you not tempted to be upset when you go to the doctor's office and have to stay in the waiting room a long time? Or to the lawyer, and you must immediately pay out the service fee? Or you go to the store and must wait in a queue a long time, only to be served with an article you really don't want but must accept because there is no time to go anywhere else? So it is in our society! If you have patience, our social system will quickly make you lose it; and if you have none, you will have to acquire it without delay through some miracle.

If then there is one virtue you must practice of necessity, it is patience. It is absolutely necessary to have patience if we are to live calmly through the various problems of life without running into greater complications and too often serious errors. Sometimes our hasty actions, made on the spur of emotional impulse, can cause us to lose the very things we love. There is a story that is illustrative. A mother kept a pet mongoose— an agile little creature with short legs and a very long, broad tail that feeds on harmful house pests—and let the little animal be a pet for her infant. The child enjoyed its nearness and played with the strange friend. One day when the mother left the house to get water, a black serpent slithered out of its hole and made straight for the child's cradle. Alerted by instinct and fearing for the life of the little one, the mongoose engaged the serpent in a fierce, bloody struggle and finally won out. Then, gratified by its heroism, the serpent's blood still dripping from its mouth, the animal ran out toward the mother to gain recognition for its bravery. At the sight of the blood-spattered mongoose the woman thought frantically that it had killed her little one, and without further reflection hurled her water-jar at the poor creature, killing it on the instant. Only when she arrived back at the house did she discover the fatal mistake she had made in her flurry of impatience. Too late did she strike her breast and vainly grieve.

There are circumstances in which not knowing how to wait can open the way to the ruin of other people. When Hannibal came down into Italy his army threw the whole of the peninsula into a frenzy of fear. The Roman general Quintus Fabius Maximus, realizing that such a formidable force could not be engaged by the unprepared troops he had at his command, employed the tactics of skirmish and withdrawal, trying to tire out the enemy without engaging in a major battle. This strategy earned for him the nickname of "Procrastinator." Public opinion held that vigorous, decisive action was needed. The Senate was influenced to depose Fabius Maximus and substitute as generals the consuls Paulus Emilius and Terence Varrus. Varrus, opposed to a policy of caution, engaged Hannibal in combat. The battle fought at Cannae was a memorable disaster which precipitated Rome into the most critical period of its history. Haste had determined the outcome. An Oriental proverb has it that "Haste is not good even to catch a fly."

Patience is likewise necessary for the accomplishment of great and lasting works. How many roads must the cyclist pedal before becoming a champion! What an expanse of sea the sailing vessel must cross before it can rest in a faraway harbor, in a friendly haven! How many centuries must pass before the mountain can emerge from the ocean! How many ages must pass before a people arrives at its authentic civilization! So too with us. A lasting good is not achieved in haste. "Though you have two good legs," an Oriental proverb reminds us, "you can climb only one tree at a time." What is genius? It is constancy in the pursuit of one goal. Johann Wolfgang Goethe spent sixty years in refining his *Faust*. Christian personality has to be developed by patience (cf. Jas. 5:7-11). The dimensions of our nature are four: intellectual, emotive, social, and religious. It is the particular task of patience to harmonize these fundamental directions of our being toward the growth and perfection of a Christian personality.

The teaching on Christian asceticism points out that this virtue of patience, like all the other virtues, can grow and be perfected. Its first stage is present under the aspect of humility, and enables us to repress movement of anger and restrain external gestures prompted by disagreeable events or words. A second phase of maturing patience brings a person to the stage of accepting contradictions, not only as a mark of self-control, but also as evidence of a desire to use these disappointments or untoward happenings as a spur and incentive for goodness and truth and as an enrichment of life.

Usually, too, the degrees of our moral perfection are acquired with patience, step by step. The seed of grace which has been sown in our souls has need of time for it to mature. "The virtues of faith, hope, and charity are increased through patience and suffering" (St. Cyprian).

For this reason Tertullian, the first to write extensively on patience, affirms that this virtue is the first characteristic of the faithful soul, just as impatience was and is the first characteristic of the devil. Tertullian, this master thinker and jurist of Carthage, makes this statement: "By the demon the world has been infested with a breath of contagious impatience, while God has initiated in it a wonderful history of patience. Evil is impatience against the good; love is patience against evil."

> O Lord God, patience, I realize, is very necessary for me, for many adverse things happen in this life. For in whatsoever way I

arrange for my peace, my life cannot be without strife and sorrow *(Imitation of Christ, Book III, Ch. 12:1)*.

Therefore, Lord, give me much patience especially when I am fatigued and tempted to rebel against so many hardships and disappointments, when I feel faint because of excessive and strenuous work, when I am discouraged by the inevitable annoyances and incomprehensions of human togetherness.

Lord, imbue me with a spirit of smiling forbearance in the face of all the trials of life, and give me the ability to accept whatever happens that is not in harmony with my way of thinking and acting.

Give me, Lord, confidence in the strife, prudence in dangers, and an uninterrupted patience in crosses, that thus I may be less unworthy of Thee, eternal and perfect Patience.

The First Duty
of Patience:
To Accept Ourselves

When we have once recognized this utter necessity of patience, without doubt we must seriously reflect upon how we can best grow in this virtue and make it effective in our lives.

The first fundamental concern of each one in this regard should be to have patience with himself. It is useless to try to support other people and the things that are not to our liking if we do not know how to control the humors of our capricious and oftentimes insidious ego.

To accept ourselves means to know how to accept the double nature of our being and our manner of acting. Greek wisdom taught that man is a microcosm, a tiny universe. Just as in the created world there are starry heavens, blossoming meadows, and fields ripe for harvest, there can also be earthquakes, devastating floods, droughts and tempests; likewise man bears within himself sublime ideals for good, and a bent for wonderful cultural projects, yet he is capable too of egoistic ideas, of error, of passion and sin. We must consider, further, that sometimes a minor matter suffices to weaken us, to make us impatient and unfeeling. It may be a glandular malfunction, a change of atmosphere, or a traumatic recollection of a past event, but it is to our own benefit to be aware of our natural and functional subjectivity. Then we can better be on guard against our passions, we can exercise ourselves in self-control, and know how to smile at our defects and mistakes.

Being patient with ourselves is, besides, accepting the characteristics we have been given by heaven. God cannot display all infinity in finite subjects such as we are; He has willed to distribute His infinite richness in the innumerable existential modulations of His creatures. For this reason, each one of us is different from every other in many ways. Every creature is a new imitation of God. It follows that an exaggerated preoccupation to be different from what God has designed us to be proves in the end to be wasted effort. On the contrary, it is an indication of good sense, as well as authentic piety, to know how to collaborate with God in developing our unique personality.

The story is told that a newly created frog turned to the good God and said to Him: "Thank You, Lord, for having made me able to leap so well!" An old proverb from southern France has the same lesson: "Has God made you a lizard? Then be content in your crevice, enjoy the rays of the sun, and thank the Lord!" A monk was asked what patience meant to him. "If I am patient," he replied, "I am satisfied with my own little cell and my own garden; I try to take care of it each day and to adapt myself to the rules of the monastery, as water adapts itself to the shape of the vessel which contains it." We have from Saint Thérèse of the Child Jesus the precious counsel: "Where the Lord has planted you, there you must blossom!"

In the vocabulary of Christian asceticism the word "patience" includes also the sense of putting up with our own imperfections. There are some Christians who regret their imperfections and lose their serenity when they discover that despite all their long-time efforts toward Christian perfection they continue to be full of faults. They need to be reminded that Christian perfection consists essentially in striving toward it. The difficulties and struggles that enter in make up part of the dynamics of the progress. For the rest, if a road is a hundred kilometers long, there is no reason to be surprised, and much less disillusioned, if on the last kilometer of the way we find the same difficulties as at the beginning. Christians, the sacred writers tell us, are disciples of Christ: so long as students remain students they have problems and always make some errors; the more they progress from grade to grade, the greater become the fatigues and mysteries of learning. It is necessary to have a continual patience with our imperfections, even moral ones, without, however, surrendering to them. The well-known Seneca, a pagan, stated: "We fight our imperfections, not to conquer them completely but to prevent them from conquering us." However fruitful a vineyard may be, it will always have some unproductive vines and some branches which must be pruned. A field might produce a rich harvest of wheat, but with all its excellence it will not be without weeds and wild grasses. Coming to the actual problem of our own striving for perfection, let us comfort ourselves with the thought that if we momentarily lose sight of the star, as happened to the three kings, it suffices that we do not lose the direction. We must be well convinced that "to set out does not mean to arrive immediately." St. Thomas, too, gives us some comfort when he tells us: "It is better to limp in the right direction than to run in the wrong direction." The Lord, who is supreme intelligence, certainly understands our situation, for He assures us that on the day of judgment we shall be rewarded equally if we have used profitably the talents He has given us.

If there is a particular time in our life when we are called upon to practice, willingly or not, heroic acts of patience, it is the period of old age, when we realize that our life is hastening on toward its close like a little paper boat a child has set upon the water of a rushing brook. We must sadly recognize that our dreams of greatness, of winning esteem, of independence, are shattered, curled up like dried leaves tossed into a bonfire. A little fable has much to teach us: "A man saw his reflection in a pool and admired himself, saying, 'I am perfect.' He followed a deer, struck him and said, 'I am strong.' He climbed a mountain, and upon reaching the peak he said, 'I am great.' He counted the stars and gave them a name and declared: 'I am intelligent.' Then he went to his room and began to ponder, and he said, 'I think, therefore I am.' On a radiant spring day he sensed the emotion of love and he sang out his joy to everyone: 'I am happy!' He dug into the earth and found gold and oil, and he concluded: 'I am rich. I have need of no one and nothing. I have everything for myself, by myself.'

"A year passed, two years, ten years, more years passed. The man returned to his pool and looked at his reflection in the water. His beauty had disappeared. He did not recognize himself anymore. He saw a deer and wanted to chase it but he had not the strength. He tried to climb the mountain but he was obliged to stay at the bottom, tired and weak. He tried to count the stars, but he could not see them very well. He felt alone, and invoked love, but he received no response. Then he had an idea. He gathered all his possessions and hastened to the market to sell them, in order to get money to buy other things that seemed beautiful. But the old things were outmoded, and the old money was valueless. Now he understood that of himself he actually possessed nothing. 'At least,' he thought, 'I have life,' and he wanted to live—but life was inexorably slipping away, like water, out of his hands. He felt himself consumed by time, ready to be consigned forever to sister death" (John Albanese).

An elderly Tuscan lady synthesized this concept and expressed it in a humorous ditty:

> What are our years?
> From 10 to 20, we are brisk as the breeze,

from 20 to 30, great strength is our ease.
From 30 to 40, we ride high on our wealth,
from 40 to 50, we lose grasp on our health.
From 50 to 60, we have dozens of ills,
from 60 and upward—then over the hills!

All this preamble has as its purpose to confirm in us the serious conviction that if we are not artists of life, managing it from our youth with a continual exercise of patience, we can hardly expect to be heroes of patience and submission when we are old, dependent and impoverished in every way. There is an art in living, but there is also an art in growing old. Jean Lamarck, the naturalist philosopher, affirmed that "the function creates the organ"; that is, practice creates in us the habit. If from our very youth we are accomplished in patience, this virtue will be our support also in our declining years.

But there is more. This our patience lived constantly, day after day, in a supernatural dimension, should be a filial response to the love of the Father; and in this way we realistically and serenely discover the role God has assigned to this period of life. John Paul II says of elderly people:

> With the wisdom and experience of their life, these aged people have entered into a period of extraordinary grace, with new possibilities

for prayer and union with God. Enriched with new spiritual strength they can place themselves at the service of others by making of their own life a fervent offering to the Lord, the Giver of life, and at the same time manifesting an appreciation of the mystery of human death. While they accept themselves realistically, they can already envision their transformation in the paschal mystery of the Lord Jesus.

This very vision—a sacred vision—will be the final stage of our existence here, to afford us tranquility and patience even in the solitude of old age, the interior synthesis of all ages. St. Teresa of Avila made this weighty statement: "God and I always form an absolute majority: with Him I fear nothing. His love is sufficient for me."

Lord, You have let this happen: I am utterly prostrate.
I have not the courage to rise, I dare not even look at You.
Nothing, I am nothing, nothing, and I know it.
Your light is terrible, Lord, and I want to run away from it.
From the day I knew You, You have illuminated my thoughts.
Your brightness penetrates them, and I see as I had never seen before.

I see the forest of my sins behind the trees
      that hide them.
I see countless roots which cannot be up-
      rooted.
I see that everything within me blocks Your
      way,
as the tiniest particle of matter blocks the sun
      and makes the night descend.
I see the demon attacking the points of my
      fortress which I deemed invulnerable.
I see myself wavering and close to falling.
I see my helplessness, I who dreamed of the
      wonderful things I would do for You.
I see that everything is confused, and not one
      of my acts is pure.
I see the infinite depths of every fault, in
      contrast to Your infinite love.
I see myself incapable of winning one single
      soul with the blast of my words and the
      pomp of my gestures.
I see the Spirit breathing where I have not
      worked, and the seed sprouting where I
      have not sown.

Nothing, nothing am I, nothing! I have
      accomplished nothing, I know it now!
But You always give light, Lord, You who
      shine upon my way.
Not a corner of my soul, of my life, remains
      in the shadow.
Wherever I turn, there is Your light—
      everywhere.
I am naked before You, Lord, and deflated.

At one time I acknowledged that I was a
    sinner, that I was unworthy;
I believed it, Lord, but I did not know it.

In Your presence I searched out for some
    faults,
but I hardly found anything to confess.
Now, Lord, my whole being kneels before
    You. I ask pardon.

Enough, Lord. I assure You that I have
    understood:
I am the nothing and You are the All.
Lord, thank You for Your light and Your
    mercy!

                                    Michel Quoist

Patience with Others

One of the greatest exercises of patience is the contact—rather the impact—with the neighbor. St. Alphonsus Liguori (died in 1787), with a colloquial homeliness to his words which is possibly a reflection of his native Naples, makes this interesting assertion: "To get along with one's neighbor five things are necessary: a glass of knowledge, a jug of wisdom, a barrel of prudence, a cask of conscience, and an ocean of patience." All this is truly necessary if we are to arrive at "possessing such an abundance of patience that we can smile even if someone steps on our corns!"

It will surely be helpful here to indicate some of the more valid and permanent motives which are useful not merely to justify but also to give effectiveness to our resolutions of patience toward the neighbor with whom we must share our life.

Like lines converging in a single point, our first remarks focus on the central theme of Christ: "I give you a new commandment, that you love one another as I have loved you" (Jn. 13:34). Christian patience is the very precision and application of this precept. "True charity cannot exist without patience, and true patience is never devoid of charity," Saint Catherine of Siena taught. In nearly all the fourteen letters of the Apostle St. Paul, he returns again and again to point out this interdependence between divine charity and patience: they are like mother and daughter, bride and handmaid, music and harmony (cf. 1 Tm. 6:11; 2 Tm. 3:10; 2 Thes. 3:5; Rom. 15; 1 Cor. 4:12; 12:4-5; Gal. 5:22; Eph. 4:26-32; Col. 3:12-13; and others).

The more we grow in charity, therefore, the more we feel the need of being patient. The story is told of two brothers who loved each other so much that for many years they lived together in one cell without ever disputing, without ever losing patience. One day one of them said to the other, "Let us also try to quarrel and lose patience with each other as other people do." "But how will we do it?" "Like this. I will place a brick here in the center of the room and say, 'This is my brick.' Then you must say, 'No, it is mine.' And then we will finish by losing our patience." He put the brick in the center of the cell and the game began. But after only a few seconds the one said to the other, "Very well, if it is yours take it, and let's be at peace!" Thus these two brothers did not succeed in losing patience with each other because, united in the Lord, they loved each other.

Another motive which advises us to be very patient toward our neighbor is the natural composition of man, ontologically body and spirit. The first pages of the Bible give us two stories of the creation of man, with different doctrinal perspectives. The first tends to underline man's greatness: he is God's masterpiece, center of the universal creation, the terminus of temporal history; as the representative of God, he is lord of all things. God said, "Let us make man in our image, after our likeness; and let them have dominion over the fish of the sea, and over the birds of the air, and over the cattle, and over all the earth, and over every creeping thing that creeps upon the earth " (Gen. 1:26-31).* It is a truly grandiose picture of pure optimism, in which man is presented from the point of view of his vocation and of the divine ideal, that is, as he should be. The second account, far from being a simple repetition of the first, with the addition of some fringes or amplifications or embellishments, presents a very different perspective. Here the sacred author presents man as originating from the slime of the earth, and his condition is, therefore, fragile, humble, earthy (cf. Gn. 2:7).

These two accounts depict clearly the ambivalence of the human creature. He can be very great in virtue and sanctity, yet he can also be entwined in ethical miseries, in errors, in sin. "How often is man crushed by his fate. How often is he a prisoner of it.... How often is he near desperation and threatened in the knowledge of the significance of his very humanity. And how often, despite all appearances, is man far from being content with himself..." (Pope John Paul II, Christmas Night, 1979).

As for ourselves, if the dynamism of charity urges us to give ourselves there where the needs are apparent, it follows that the irritating qualities of our neighbor—imaginary or real—far from being a stimulus to unpleasant reaction, must rather be an appeal for self-giving—"compassion" in the etymological sense of the word, that is, sharing in the miseries of others. There are two types of patience: one purely human, which finds its justification in the merits or importance of the other, and one authentically Christian, which prompts us to involve ourselves in the distress of our brother who is weighted with sorrows or moral shortcomings.

Another claim to our indulgence and patience with regard to those who seem to drain our reserve of calmness and serenity by their defects is the conviction that we, too, are

weak and not without imperfections. Some
exegetes interpret in this vein a parable of our
Lord (cf. Mt. 7:3-5). Two neighbors both had a
cistern closed with beams to prevent any
objects from falling into the water. But now
into one of these cisterns falls a piece of wood
that was covering it, while into the other falls
an entire beam, perhaps disintegrated by the
weather. Jesus concludes the parable by telling His listeners that the one man, before
disparaging the other because of the splinter
that fell into his well, should rather take
cognizance of the beam that has fallen into his
own. An Oriental proverb says it well: "Before
complaining about how dirty the city is, each
citizen should tidy up his own house." One
day Paul Claudel admonished a lad who
lamented that he was not accepted by the
others: "My boy, do not be too greatly disturbed about not being understood by the
others; rather ask yourself what you are doing
to understand and support your compan-
ions." St. Paul in his clear and effective style
recommends to all to "bear one another's
burdens" (cf. Gal. 6:2).

Without wanting to elaborate new theories but simply to arouse within ourselves
stronger motives for the achievement of
Christian aims in our dialogue, it will be
helpful to point out that every antagonist we
have, even the most wicked, may give us the

surprise of a sudden unexpected conversion, for the power of divine grace touches where it will. It is for us, then, to recognize God's hand and His moment.

The person who intends to have a talk with someone whose character is not recognized as very good should present himself as one who knows and understands the complexities of the other, appreciates the good qualities which perhaps are not openly evident, and also is aware of the inner stress which prompts the unfriendly attitude. Any adversary we may have, furthermore, never ceases to be a person and therefore worthy of our comprehension and esteem. Dialogue and understanding will be possible only if there are no impassable barriers between two contenders; they must rather be animated by benevolence and sincerity if they desire to avoid a clash that will oppress their human and Christian sensitivity.

Another motive to stimulate us to patience with our neighbor is the conviction that contact with others is the test and the means of our greater spiritual advancement. Virtue is acquired through the presence of its opposite. St. Augustine tells us: "There are evil people in the world so that the patience of the virtuous will be tried and augmented." And St. Francis de Sales in his turn offers this exhortation: "To accept the imperfections of our neighbor is one of the chief signs of our love for him."

One day St. Philip Neri (1515-1595), who was called the Apostle of Rome, lamented to the Lord because he had to treat with an impertinent and bothersome person. He heard an interior voice admonishing him: "Philip, you have asked me for patience. This is the way to acquire it!"

A final thought to be considered is that true dialogue requires calmness, composure, patience. One who lets nervous tension overcome him is hardly able to distinguish things properly; it is like trying to look through binoculars held in palsied hands, or attempting to thread a needle while dancing. This truth is of such great importance that not a few physicians prefer to call in a different doctor to tend their sick wife or children, fearing that their affection and tension might impede an objective diagnosis. It is said that Julius Caesar, a volatile person, had the habit of counting to twenty before giving an answer, especially if his nerves were strained or he was irritated. It is always necessary to know how to be patient in answering, but doubly so when the dialogue is controversial and emotional. Patience is necessary to know how to speak the truth at the right moment and to the right persons.

Our topic broadens here to include in our patient relations with our neighbor even the kind of patience we need for the interpretation of history and the sometimes strange doings of our society. Occasionally we feel inclined to condemn the world, the government, the labor system, and social or political organizations because things are not going the way we feel they should go; problems are not being resolved according to the design we have mentally mapped out for their solution. Even admitting the freedom we have to criticize the inertia of public servants or urge the correction of some wrong they may have done, still we must never forget that the attainment of peace requires calmness, discretion and time. History unravels slowly, involved as it is with countless human interests, vileness and weakness. To take cognizance of this is an act of good sense and of truthfulness.

Furthermore, it is not for us to disdain the universe, for after all these eons it has not yet been rejected by God. An Oriental sage, the Indian poet Tagore, Nobel prize winner in literature for 1913, comforted his countrymen by writing: "Every child born into the world is an announcement of joy, because it is a sign that God is not yet tired of man." Neither let us forget that the world existed before we were born, and when we die this very world we are so prone to belittle will continue its march without us, and perhaps it will get along better than it did when we were present.

We believe we can synthesize this lesson of patience with a counsel dictated to us by a tribal chieftain of Madagascar, a large island in the Indian Ocean: "If you have quarrelled with a brother and intend to kill him, first sit down, fill your pipe and smoke. When you have finished you will realize that the death penalty is too severe a punishment for the fault he has committed, and you will settle to give him a few strokes instead. But fill your pipe a second time and smoke it to the end. When it is finished you will have persuaded yourself that instead of strokes, some reproofs would be sufficient. Then after you have filled your pipe a third time and smoked it to the end, you will be convinced that the best thing to do is to go to that brother and embrace him." It is a fact of experience: the more we advance in years and in life, the more we are disposed to be indulgent. Perhaps for this very reason God is all goodness—He is eternal.

But the learning and imitation of Oriental wisdom is not the driving force of the Christian. He knows that history is dominated and vivified by the death and resurrection of Christ, and he is equally certain that the greatest victories, even in the social world, are realized in self-sacrifice and the exercise of mercy. The true follower of Christ finds his peace in living according to the exhortation St. Paul addressed to the Christians of his day:

> We put no obstacle in any one's way, so that no fault may be found with our ministry, but as servants of God we commend ourselves in every way: through great endurance, in afflictions, hardships, calamities, beatings, imprisonments, tumults, labors, watching, hunger; by purity, knowledge, forbearance, kindness, the Holy Spirit, genuine love, truthful speech, and the power of God; with the weapons of righteousness for the right hand and for the left; in honor and dishonor, in ill repute and good repute. We are treated as impostors, and yet are true; as unknown, and yet well known; as dying, and behold we live; as punished, and yet not killed; as sorrowful, yet always rejoicing; as poor, yet making many rich; as having nothing, and yet possessing everything.
>
> (2 Cor. 6:3-10)*

With the intention of clinching the leading thoughts of this meditation, we offer here a decalogue of patience. It should prove helpful in moments of interior tension and social friction, and it can be a handy service for those engaged in vigorous apostolic activity.

Decalogue of Patience

1. Sweetness, gentleness and patience are the complement of the virtue of fortitude and the mark of an authentic Christian personality. Always be kind: "Nothing calms an infuriated elephant more quickly than the sight of a meek lamb" (St. Francis de Sales).

2. When a child is born, weakness is born. Genius is merely some filled-in gaps of ignorance. A saint is a person who has fewer defects than others. If the good things of a neighbor give us reason to love him, his defects should be a motive to love him even more.

3. Do not become annoyed at human weaknesses and foibles. We have two hands, two legs, two eyes, two ears—but only one liver. Let us not spoil it with things we cannot change. Many situations improve by themselves. Time is the best secretary for goodness and truth.

4. To love is to let oneself be wounded. A person who reacts to every criticism or contradiction by giving brusque answers and losing patience shows that he is incapable of improvement and will never learn the art of being a man.

5. Persons who are mean, bitter, quarrelsome already have much to suffer because of their character. Do not be too harsh with

them! To be annoyed with the weak is to give proof of not being strong: it would be like getting angry at the desert for not having water. To be understanding, however, is an encouragement for the other.

6. Often the person who does wrong is weak rather than evil; therefore experience and philosophy ought to lead to patience and longanimity. Otherwise they are rather useless, not to say even harmful.

7. Insults, quarrels and murmurings are the arguments of those who are at fault; and noise is the fault of those who have no arguments.

8. Learn from nature and the countryside to be patient. Be able to wait, and conquer evil with good (cf. Rom. 12:21). The meek are not those who surrender but those who fight evil with the violence of love.

9. The learned person sees everything with the eyes of science, the politician with the eyes of the party, but the Christian sees people and things with the eyes of the light of God's mercy.

10. Man speaks. An outpouring of words: "Peace—liberty—solidarity—dreams." God speaks: "Love one another." Only one word, but capable of changing the world.

There comes to mind as a final resolution the words of St. Augustine: "Love and do as

you please. If you are silent, be silent out of
love. If you speak, speak out of love. If you
admonish, admonish because you love. If you
pardon, pardon because you love. Let there
be in you the root of love, for from this root
can proceed nothing but good!" (Tract on
St. John 7:8)

Lord, how other people weigh upon me!
How disappointing, capricious, egoistic I find
    them!
But You desire that instead of cursing the
    darkness
I light a candle with the flame of Your love.

Lord, You have placed me among others
not to set me against them or above them
but to have me go about among them,
to be for them, to love You in them.
Lord, You desire that I, too, in imitation of
    You,
believe in my brother, respect his life and his
    opinion,
support him in his weakness.
Give me, Lord, a clear vision,
that I may perceive in my brother Your divine
    countenance
and your supernal nobility.

Truly, how beautiful it is for us to be
    together, Lord,
to be brother to one another, in divine
    communion,
and to walk together toward You, the only
    Love of the world!

Patience Has
Its Summit in Pardon

The greatest manifestation of the mercy of God toward us is His pardon. Similarly, the pardon which every Christian is called upon to grant to his brother is the vertex of our human and fraternal solidarity and patience.

Let us reflect together on some motives which must impel us to practice this "audacious policy of pardon" (Paul VI, April 15, 1973), as we recall a Swedish proverb: "He who pardons is already sufficiently vindicated."

Without a long preamble we begin immediately by noting that pardon belongs not only to the essence of charity but also to our supernatural perfection and holiness. This sanctity is the goal of our actual striving to imitate the heavenly Father who diffuses mercy. We read in the Gospel: "As the Father makes his sun to rise upon the good and the wicked, and sends the rain upon the just and the unjust, as he pardons all and is merciful toward the ingrate and the sinner—so also should you seek to be perfect as he is" (cf. Mt. 5:43ff.; Lk. 6:35-38).

Evidently we cannot imitate the Father in all His attributes. He is the Infinite. For this reason God in His wisdom and comprehension invites us to be imitators of Him in diffusing love and pardon. And God is so *direct* and *resolute* with us that in the final scrutiny on the day of judgment we shall be examined precisely on this point; that is, we shall be judged on our charity. We read this in a pointed and convincing manner in the Gospel of St. Matthew (cf. Mt. 25:31-46).

The Lord Jesus holds us so insistently to this our mutual pardon that, after having taught the Apostles the prayer of the Pater Noster, He followed it with the one sole catechetical clarification:

> If you forgive men their trespasses, your heavenly Father also will forgive you; but if you do not forgive men their trespasses, neither will your Father forgive your trespasses.
> (Mt. 6:14-15)*

The passport to paradise, then, the "homeland of the forgiven," consists in having shown mercy and pardon to our neighbor. Jesus tells us further: An unmerciful servant was forgiven a debt of ten thousand talents by his master, but later this same servant was severely punished because he in his turn did not forgive and condone the debt of his friend, an insignificant sum of a few dollars. The conclusion is clear: only in pardoning and canceling our neighbor's debt can we obtain infinite mercy. "Pardon and you will be pardoned," the Lord often repeats to us (cf. Mt. 18:23ff.; 6:14).

As a pastoral note a consoling thought of Don Pietro Berruti, a Salesian priest, may be helpful here: "Many of us might be tormented by an anxiety: 'At the moment of my death, will I be in the grace of God and worthy of Him? Can I be at ease despite my many sins? Has the Lord really pardoned me for them all?' But let us listen to what Jesus has to say: 'Forgive, and you will be forgiven.' Oh, what a powerful word of comfort and hope is this! Therefore let us forgive, let us forget, let us not retrace all the crooked ways, let us not demand payment.... Let us smile at the person who complains, serve the one who deserts. Let us show benevolence and amiability to the rude and antagonistic person, or the one who inveighs against us. Let us be patient with all. Ah, what fortitude this demands! Certainly. It costs very much to love with the heart of Jesus, but how consoling are His words: 'Forgive and be forgiven.'"

In one of his keen intuitions Tertullian assures us that God is the depository of the patience and pardon we give to our brethren.

He preserves our every gesture in this direction to reward it with the hundredfold in eternity. St. Peter Chrysologus, doctor of the Church and bishop of Ravenna in the fifth century, known as "the golden-tongued" because of his eloquence, tells us: "Whatever you give in mercy returns in abundance to your own provision. Therefore, in order that you may not have to lose by wanting to keep for yourself, give freely to others and then you will reap.... The manner in which you desire to have mercy shown to you must be your manner of showing mercy to others; the abundance of mercy you desire for yourself must be your abundance of mercy for others; offer promptly the same mercy you desire for yourself." The measure of mercy which distances us from others is the measure of our distance from God.

Among the motives which induce us to create within ourselves a generous incentive to pardon, there may not be lacking the conviction that we are all involved in a common solidarity of misery and sin. An Oriental proverb admonishes us that one who does not pardon destroys the bridge he himself must pass over. Sooner or later, for some reason or other, we all have need of the pardon of our neighbor. No one of us can ever believe himself so perfect that he needs no support and pardon from his brothers. And if—as hypothesis—an offended Christian does not want to forgive on the presumption that he is innocent, then there would be not just one sinner but two: the one who offended the first, and the one who would not forgive.

But the true follower of Christ knows how to conquer by pardoning. He knows how to transform the offense as an oyster transforms into pearls the wound it receives. Like a flower trampled upon by passers-by, the forgiving person sublimates his vengeance by perfuming with fragrance the offender and the environment. A poet sings:

> Doing good to those who hurt us
> is like the blossoming almond tree
> When it is struck with a stone
> it sheds a shower of snowy petals.

Psychological studies have shown it to be true that forgiveness offered by one who has been offended often creates in the heart of the adversary a movement of contrition and goodness. This fact, which we cannot disregard as a motive for offering pardon, is expressed also in Sacred Scripture, which invites us to treat our enemy as a friend, "heaping glowing coals of patient charity upon his head" (cf. Prv. 25:21-22; Rom. 12:20-21). To better convince his hearers that loving patience always wins the victory, St. Peter Damian told this story: "The wind and the sun contested between themselves to see which one of the two could succeed in making a traveler take off his hat. The wind blew violently, but the man managed to keep his hat on his head by holding it down firmly with both hands. Then it was the sun's turn. Without noise but with luminous patience the sun began to pour its warmth upon the traveler with ever-increasing strength. Finally the poor fellow, bathed in perspiration, had to yield and take his hat off his head bacause it was too hot.'' It is quite true that when a prodigal son is made the object of mercy he does not feel humiliated; rather, he is given new self-respect and new courage (cf. *Dives in misericordia*, no. 6). Surely these thoughts urge us to a resolution, one which St. Paul has already formulated for us: "Be kind to one another, tenderhearted, forgiving one another, as God in Christ forgave you. Therefore be imitators of God, as beloved children. And walk in love, as Christ loved us and gave himself up for us, a fragrant offering and sacrifice to God" (Eph. 4:32; 5:1-2).*

We cannot conclude this chapter without recording the wonderful example of pardon we have seen in Pope John Paul II. Seriously wounded in Piazza San Pietro on that awful Wednesday, May 13, 1981, by a Turk, the youthful Mehmet Ali Agca, the Supreme Pontiff expressed his sentiments in the first brief discourse he gave from his room in the Gemelli Hospital: "I pray for the brother who has struck me, whom I have sincerely pardoned."

Lord, You are Love. You have told me so
      repeatedly in the Gospel.
You made me understand it when You described Yourself as Father
and as the Good Shepherd in search of the
      lost sheep.
Give me the grace to believe in Your love,
      to be a joy-filled apostle of Your infinite
      mercy, aware that the most lasting victories are obtained only through patience
      and pardon.
Lord Jesus, You have shown Your love for us
      by sacrificing Yourself
on the cross, and from the heights
      of Calvary You have diffused pardon
      throughout the world.
Grant that the ardent charity and indulgence
      You manifested
may be also my way, my ideal, my victory.
O Holy Spirit, enlighten and convert
my heart, invade my soul,
so that my pathway may be that of bringing
      light and comfort,
that my life may be one with my wounded
      brethren whom I meet on the way,
and that I may be hope for those who offend
      Your merciful love.
Thank You, Lord!

Crucified Patience: Suffering

Our response to the goodness and long-suffering of the Lord must include above all a firm determination and resolution to maintain a conscious patience in the face of two great mysteries of life: suffering and infirmity, in which, as St. Augustine says, "patience is crucified."

Let us meditate upon each of these two themes, and at the end draw from our considerations some practical rules of behavior for exercising ourselves in patience whenever we may find ourselves in a condition of suffering or infirmity.

It is a commonplace statement that every life is interwoven with sorrow. "When I was born a voice said to me: 'You are born to bear the cross.' Weeping, I embraced the cross heaven laid upon me. Then I looked, looked, looked: everyone down here is bearing a cross!" Sorrow is like a garment; whether it is one color or another, everyone must wear it.

An Indian proverb spells it out like this: "One day is in your favor, another day will be against you." Thus our existence could be compared, in effect, to an airship which has to make scheduled flights: sometimes it meets skies limpid and clear as cobalt or at other times heavy with fog, and encounters impetuous winds and storms as well as the furthering jet stream. Sorrow—sickness—death: these are the currency each one of us must pay out, sooner or later. To surmount suffering we must surmount life.

If this is so, man's duty is not exhausted in the perfecting of his capacity for culture, labor, technology, social amenities and love; he must also fortify himself by learning how to suffer. We must all advance in the art of patience according to the teaching which comes from above.

Christ did not eliminate suffering, nor did He propound a philosophy of evil or a theology of sorrow. Rather, He transformed our sorrow and, by living it in the first person, He weighted it with sublime ideals of love, of perfection, of supernatural hope. We must be convinced that even the cross has its radiance, that it is a tree which can produce good and abundant fruits; the Son of God chose it as a throne from which to give us life, as a pulpit from which to tell us of His infinite love. It is not for the Christian, then, to be repeatedly seeking a divine explanation, spasmodically beating at heaven's door with the question, "Why, O Lord, are you sending me this trial?" It is for him, rather, to try to make of every hardship a divine benefit. Actually, though sorrow or suffering in itself has a negative quality: evil, diminution of strength either physical or spiritual, it may also be indirectly the basis of a vital process at all levels.

Now if we take time to investigate some positive points as we reflect on the problem of suffering, we note first of all that the life of man is enriched with ethical coloring and moral growth precisely through the trials that have to be faced. One who does not know how to suffer remains psychologically a child. True life is born in sorrow. Leonardo da Vinci, echoing a statement of Homer, expressed this thought in memorable words: "God gives everything to man, but at the cost of exertion; on every beautiful thing in this world there must fall the fecundity of tears." Pleasure itself is true not when it is sought volup-tuously as the primary scope of action, but only when it is the consequence of our dona-tion and sacrifice: it is suffering which makes pleasure more pleasing.

Marc Lorenzi sings:

> To understand the gifts of morning
> I passed through the darkness of night;

to capture the sweetness of spring
I suffered the long frosts of winter;
to learn what true friendship is
I endured the restraint of solitude;
to grasp and enjoy hope
I carried the cross.

We shall not be too impatient in the face of sorrow if we consider further that this inseparable companion of our existence can strengthen us from within for greater conquests. Time and again man feels the urge to review the structuring of his own activity: he tends to question all the acquired certainties in order to explore new theories of progress and of social solidarity. Without this process there surely would never have been the forward march of civilization, nor the thrust of the sciences or of technical development, much less the urge toward the formation of one universal family. Man is by vocation a being who must go beyond himself and, paradoxically, this happens through sorrow. Animals must be aggressive and defensive to maintain themselves in life; the struggles of man against difficulties, threats of harm or other hardships, can serve to develop him spiritually. One of the arts of Providence in our regard is that of letting us find treasures of salvation in the very experience of certain evils which make us suffer much, and of giving us a taste for new things, most useful in difficult and painful situations, which we do not want to accept. In the words of Luigi Veuillot, "There are benedictions of God which.enter the house by breaking the windows." And St. Paul assures us: "We know that by turning everything to their good, God cooperates with all those who love him" (Rom. 8:28).

Our reserve of patience in suffering can be increased if we keep in mind that sorrow is often God's missionary. Suffering, the void within and around us, produces in the soul an immense desert. Affliction makes us realize that we are poor creatures exposed to risks, insecure beings, greatly in need of help. From this negative state of impotence and fear there can emerge the voice and the appeal of One who is Strength *par excellence,* the Unchangeable, the source of every gift and every help. Thus, our misery can touch supreme wealth, our solitude can be populated by the presence of God very close and intimate as Father and Shepherd, and our sorrow can lead us to love divine love. The history of not a few converts demonstrates that not rarely sorrow has been the road the Lord chose to lead many pilgrim souls to Himself. The Book of Tobias tells us that when the good man was close to the Lord it was necessary that he be tried in the crucible of suffering (cf. Tb. 12:13, Douay Edition). And the Apostle Peter reminds us that whoever enters the household of God must be purified to be rendered worthy of Him; the one who suffers for being a Christian should thank God that he has been called (cf. 1 Pt. 4:17).

Is it not sorrow which makes of us true followers of Christ? The vocation to Christian election consists not only in morals, sentiment and affections; its highest expression is our assimilation to the Crucified. Woodsmen tell us that when a branch is thrown on the fire it releases the colors which have penetrated it: the black of night, the purple of morning, the red of sunset, the silver of the stars. It is precisely in difficult moments that the true follower of Christ reveals his loyalty and adherence to the One who said: "If anyone wants to be a follower of mine, let him...take up his cross every day and follow me" (Lk. 9:23). For the Christian, then, sufferings and trials are not a handicap in his profession of faith, but on the contrary they are the certificate of recognition of his interior authenticity.

Our patience in moments of sorrow will grow even more if we look upon suffering as an educational prerequisite for understanding our neighbor better and loving him more. If it is true that without love one cannot live, it is likewise true that without sorrow one cannot love. It is necessary to have suffered to be able to share intimately in the sufferings of others. If one has suffered, his participation in the pain of others is not pure philanthropy or convenience; it is an affectionate, sincere, full, comforting communication. Joy unites us, but sorrow binds us more profoundly. It is not without reason that great friendships have their origin in sorrow suffered together. Sometimes many years are needed for us to go out of ourselves to approach the needs of our neighbor, but there are times when one great suffering suffices to shorten by miles and miles the distance to the neighbor's soul. Here, too, patience—the capacity to accept and transform sorrow, becomes fruitful in love and the bright bringer of goodness.

To conclude, let us briefly add that this our "crucified patience" is the means and the guarantee of arriving at the glory of the resurrection. In the letter to the Hebrews it is expressly stated: "You will need endurance to do God's will and gain what he has promised" (10:36), and this thought is reiterated in many other scriptural passages (cf. Heb. 12:11-12; 2 Cor. 4:8-12; Rom. 5:3-5; 8:17; 2 Tm. 2:11-12). "To attain this end," St. Francis de Sales tells us, "one ounce of patience in suffering is more valuable and more precious than a pound of action." It is interesting to note that

the Greek Bible expresses the mystical richness of suffering patience with the word
ipomoné, a concept very dear also to Saint
Catherine of Siena.

We have offered in these pages some
thoughts on the theme of sorrow or suffering,
but we do not presume to have explained it
fully. Sorrow will always remain a mystery to
us. Every word that is said about it, however
learned and profound, will remain quite inadequate; every response, however pedantic,
will be nothing but childish prattle, lacking
clarity and logic. We have only glimpsed some
ray of light, some pulsation of life, sufficient
however to convince us that sorrow, too, has
its mission in the world, its reason to be, its
spiritual richness. If we were to peruse a page
written in a foreign language unknown to us,
we may perhaps understand an expression
here and there, but we should be incapable of
grasping the meaning of all the words. Likewise in this matter of suffering. Let us think of
it as a letter sent to us by a Friend, with a
message well thought out, logical and assur-
ing, but escaping our comprehension.

On the other hand, it is not absolutely
necessary that we understand everything
about our being, nor is it indispensable that
the page of our life be written according to our
tastes and expectations. The only important

thing is to realize that the cross can be for us a
school and a pathway to virtue, that the
Father loves us despite our not understanding
His plan for us—is to discover that God's love
is the basis of everything and the terminus of
every situation. Let us never forget that God is
"a faithful God, without unfairness" (Dt.
32:4), and that "everything that we see, He
has already seen before us!" (Pope John XXIII)

Heavenly Father, walk with us as You once
walked with the Hebrews.
Never let us believe that we have become too
big to pay attention to Your direction
but grant that we grow in conformity to it,
that we flourish under it,
like the good grain which grows patiently in
the field;
grant that we may never forget how much
You have done for us.

Heavenly Father, You speak to men in many
ways.
You speak even when You are silent, so that
when You speak with words the
moment of understanding may be even more
intimate.
May Your silence be blessed, Lord, as are all
the words You address to men.

Grant that men may never forget that You
speak to them as well in silence.
To the person who is waiting for You and
Your silent message, give the

consolation of understanding that You are
silent out of love, just as You
speak out of love. Whether You are silent or
speak in words, You guide the
one who hears Your voice or Your silence.
May he always know that for him
You are the same Father!

Sören Kierkegaard

Sickness: a Second Great Mystery of Patience

All that we have said about the bond between patience and suffering seems to expand to greater horizons as we set about considering motivations for accepting illness, big sister of suffering and trial, very perilous for our human and divine destinies. Like every other suffering, illness is an ambivalent reality: it can completely destroy our happiness, radically crush our ideal; or, seen from a Christian point of view and accepted with the grace of God, it can make us grow in human qualities and in sanctity.

In this life we all have a tendency to put a mask upon ourselves, cherishing the illusion of being great, infallible, exceptional, invulnerable, almost eternal. Illness brings us brusquely to the truth and constrains us to touch with our own hand our littleness and creaturely poverty. Thus almost forcibly brought back to our objective value as limited and fragile creatures, we can humbly begin to reconstruct a new path toward terrestrial realities, toward our brothers, and above all toward the Lord. As we look at it this way, sickness cannot be considered as a condition ascribed to converging pathogenic elements in our organism, nor as a period of our existence in which our body and our spirit are not functioning as they ought, but rather as a propitious time for the better centering of our purpose and more authentically adhering to the real values of life and of the spirit.

We immediately state our premise that because life is a value and a gift of God, it is the duty of the sick person to collaborate in the recovery of his health and vigor. The Christian invalid does not accept illness passively, stoically; insofar as he is able, he acts in two directions: in the first place, he sincerely fights with all his strength, in conjunction with the healing powers of men and of God, that his malady may be definitely overcome; secondly, he sublimates his illness, channeling it into a source of moral and spiritual strength. In this two-dimensional activity, human and spiritual, patience succeeds in reconciling the will of God with the divergent claims of virtue and the desire for recovery; it likewise becomes a dynamic means and manner of growth and maturity in personality. "Life is great," said Pope Paul VI, "for what we suffer, for what we love, and for what we overcome'' (October 2, 1963).

Still more. The sick person may enter into the privileged zone of familiarity and friendship with God, who has a predilection for the humble, the infirm, the "poor." In the Christian mystique, every sick person represents the new humanity exposed completely to grace, prone before the Lord to be permeated unconditionally by His presence. The sick person expresses in himself the supernatural vocation to a mystery of life and glory, a free gift of the Lord, whose power of love and mercy shines out especially there where the need is greater and the human void is more vast.

In the vocabulary of the Church, which is of course the vocabulary of God, the sick person is also regarded as a close collaborator of Christ for the triumph of His kingdom of mercy. It is precisely the infirm who, reduced to inactivity in the visible world, become the silent workers in the invisible world of the Mystical Body of Christ. Participating so genuinely in the cross of Jesus and almost blending their countenance with that of the Crucified, they merit to cooperate in a greater shower of grace and of sanctity for the benefit of the people of God. For this reason the Magisterium of the Church, most recently through John Paul II, defines the sick as "the most vital and dynamic part of the ecclesial apostolate. The Church has need of the sick" (John Paul II, January 23, 1981: Hospital, Island of Guam, Micronesia).

This same Holy Father, "Papa Wojtyla," expressed his sentiments in this way during his painful stay in the Polyclinic Agustino Gemelli: "I desire today to address myself in a special manner to the sick, as an invalid like them, offering them a word of comfort and of hope. The day after my election to the Chair of Peter I came to the Gemelli Polyclinic for a visit; at that time I stated that I wished to support my papal ministry pre-eminently through those who suffer. Providence has disposed that I return to the polyclinic as a patient. I reaffirm now my convictions of that time: suffering accepted in union with the sufferings of Christ has incomparable efficacy for accomplishing the divine design of salvation. I will repeat here with St. Paul:

> It makes me happy to suffer for you, as I am suffering now, and in my own body to do what I can to make up all that has still to be undergone by Christ for the sake of his body, the Church.
>
> (Col. 1:24)

"I invite all the sick to unite themselves with me in offering to Christ their sufferings for the good of the Church and of humanity. May Mary most holy be our support and our comfort..." (May 24, 1981).

Furthermore, through his manner the sick person can give the most beautiful example of how to believe, how to hope, and how to love the Lord and His Church. Christian courage does not consist in making noise, of advertising the good news of Christ when life is rosy and everything is going fine, but rather in being disciples, followers and witnesses of Christ despite all the difficulties of life and of sickness. When the French convert, the writer Joris Karl Huysmans (1907), learned that he was suffering from cancer of the tongue, it is said that he exclaimed: "I must suffer now so that those who read my writings may know that my Catholicism has not been mere literature."

The invalid who gives Christian witness of smiling serenity despite all his pain and debility can have a tremendous apostolic effect upon people who are enjoying good health. A sick woman, Katy Canevaro, tells of herself: "Often people who are well have no joy. They give no thought to how wonderful it is to be healthy, alive! It has been my resolution to remind them, to urge them to enjoy life, to rejoice, using my own infirmity for this purpose.... I have learned that there is an indirect means of announcing to the brethren that there can be joy in the world, and I want to make them conscious of it. Therefore I began to smile and to diffuse my part of joy, that portion which every creature has received from the good God to communicate to others. This has meant a new life for me also: my illness has been transformed into an agreeable and easy task, and from my bed, as from a monstrance, there must radiate invisible rays of goodness, of confidence, of humility, of gratitude, of hope, of eternity. But what counted above all was my smile. It was then that I became truly patient."

But the crowning verity of the sick person's patience is his hope of reward. By the very fact of his infirmity the invalid thinks continually of a better human future after his recovery. On this future, relative to his physical health, he can well insert the thought of the future glory and beatitude which the Lord has implanted as a supernatural instinct in every heart. Then, too, the many cures accomplished by Christ should be seen not only as the alleviation and recovery of the sick but principally as a sure indication to the Hebrews that the eschatological and Messianic age had begun, the definitive perfection of which would come only when time would be no more. Then there would be complete abolition of sorrow, of grief and mourning, of infirmity.

And if Jesus chose to work many of His miracles on the Sabbath, it was to remind His hearers of the great eternal Sabbath where every evil would be conquered and every sorrow requited.

So it is. Hellenic wisdom saw in patience a means of maintaining a certain human dignity, but Christian wisdom has made of it a virtue which will help us "lose ourselves" in a victory of love and future glory. The promised merit buoys us up. In his first letter St. Peter tells us: "For what credit is it, if when you do wrong and are beaten for it you take it patiently? But if when you do right and suffer for it you take it patiently, you have God's approval " (1 Pt. 2:20).*

Unfortunately the modern world is a slave of technology and material things. It has neither the time nor the will to think of heaven and to entertain supernatural hope. But there are and always will be the poor, the afflicted, the sick who, rooted in the word of the Lord, know how to hope with "persevering patience" (cf. Rom. 5:5), for the kingdom of heaven. It is they, the sick and the suffering, who have set out on the "narrow way" to enter more easily into the kingdom of heaven (cf. Lk. 13:24).

Let us listen to a simple and graceful bit of poetry, fascinating as a chain of pearls. It was written by Father John Bigozzi, a Jesuit of Monte Sansovino (Arezzo). When he learned that he was gravely ill he sent to a friend a consoling letter in which these precious lines were enshrined:

> My suffering is a little golden key.
> Little, yes, but it unlocks a great treasury.
> It is a cross, but the cross of Jesus:
> When I embrace it I no longer feel it.
> I have not counted the days of suffering;
> I know that Jesus has written them in His
>   heart.
> I live moment for moment,
> and then the day passes as if it were an hour.
> They have told me that—seen from up
>   there—
> a whole life appears to be but a moment.

St. Ignatius, martyred in Rome about 107, exclaimed: "How beautiful it is to experience the sunset of life's day on earth, to arise in the dawn of God!"

> Lord, deliver me from the tormenting temptation of looking upon illness as a useless part of life, as a failure of my existence, a period empty and valueless. May I accept the cross of illness, Lord, knowing that before You nothing is lost.
>   Reveal to me, O Lord, the meaning of this my suffering. When I was well, I often confused virtue with the state of physical

well-being, contentment, and the satisfaction of one who has everything. Illness makes me touch the depths of my misery: because of this, I am more convinced that I have great need of Your infinite mercy.

Lord, grant that I may accept solitude without burdening others with the cross that weighs upon me, the cross that is really my glory. Never permit me to feel sorry for myself or to have excessive fear of what may happen to me, for only thus will I be able to look to You with confidence and contribute to the serenity of those who are round about me.

A Response
to Some Objections

We are not unaware that in presenting these thoughts on suffering and illness we may have stressed unduly a more optimistic outlook, even to the point of seeming naive. But "if the future belongs to the optimist," we feel we have not done wrong in offering a restraint for feelings of desperation when we are beset with affliction. In this conference, however, we want to be more practical by offering some positive and helpful methods so that "our patience be always a companion to our hope" (cf. Rom. 8:24-25).

The first resolution we must make when we are ill or afflicted is that of collaborating from the outset in the efforts made to preserve our life and our health. According to Saint Bernard of Clairvaux (1091-1153) there are four steps to Christian love: first, to love oneself because of one's own person; second, to love oneself for love of God; third, to love God because this is His loving will; and fourth, to love oneself as the object of the love of God, whose benevolence embraces all His creatures.

God is interested in our life and our health. He is the God of life and not of death, of joy and not of sorrow. The salvation which God offers to us is not partial and only heavenly; it includes also the earthly, the cosmic aspect. Eschatology is not a devaluation of terrestrial realities but an integration of our present history with what is to be. In this perspective it is easy to see how God can will that we endeavor to combat suffering and sickness, for in themselves these realities tend to lessen or destroy our physical and psychic personality. To learn to dominate the earth and its harmful elements is a divine command which we must obey in all its ramifications (cf. Gn. 1:28). It is quite true that the Lord tells us to carry our cross, but He does not tell us to go out and look for it or to bear it passively (cf. Mt. 16:24).

A second attitude to assume in the midst of a trial is the hope that things can change by the very strength of our good will and cooperation. Even though man is influenced genetically as Darwin teaches, economically and historically as Karl Marx thinks, and psychologically as Sigismund Freud writes, he can nevertheless be capable, under the influence of divine grace, of overcoming certain stages of physical or psychic ill-being and discover in himself new potentialities. We have the story of Patrick, aged 24. A bullet, accidentally shot from a pistol, became lodged in his spinal column and confined him to a bed with no hope of recovery. This young athlete saw himself severed from the world and from normal persons in the very flower of his young manhood. But at all costs Patrick wanted to succeed in life. By exerting to the full his strong will he became a photographer; he travels around the world in a special cart. He has recorded his experiences (cf. Segal, Patrick: *Life Can Begin Again)* in order to show that it is possible to be victorious over misadventure.

One who surrenders never conquers, and one who conquers never surrenders. Richard of St. Victor writes: "Take a step, try your strength, put your hand to the work, begin—and God will do the rest." The American psychologist William James has this counsel: "If every day you do two things you do not like to do, gradually you will attain a self-mastery that will help you respond properly when you are faced with unexpected difficulties."

Another simple method of remaining calm and patient in sorrow and infirmity is to live one day at a time. A person who has an exaggerated preoccupation about how things will go in the future cannot escape a paralyzing agony. And this for three reasons: because it is impossible to decipher and attack those distressing representations, probable or imaginary, projected into the future and outside the dominion of men; because such preoccupations, accumulating with time, come to be amassed mysteriously into one great sorrow which is beyond the daily capacity to suffer; and, finally, because the Lord gives His grace each time for the present difficulties, not the future ones: "...tomorrow will take care of itself. Each day has enough trouble of its own," Jesus tells us in His Gospel (Mt. 6:34). When Paul of Tarsus was oppressed with anxiety the same Lord answered him: "My grace is enough for you" (2 Cor. 12:9). It is prudent, then, to bear our daily cross and to advance step by step on the sorrowful way of our life. The story is told of a hospitalized patient who had both his arms and his leg in a cast. Nevertheless he was always in a joyful mood. A neighboring patient asked him how long he would have to bear this immobility. He replied: "Only one day at a time, or better, one hour at a time of the 168 hours that make up a week." The Servant of God, Fr. James Alberione, told his spiritual sons and daughters: "The Lord illumines the way little by little as one moves ahead; he does not light all the lamps at once, at the outset, when they are not needed, but rather at the proper moment, so as not to waste light."

Another Christian doctrine is that God does not permit our suffering to be greater than our strength, and that He gives His help and comfort at the opportune moment (cf. 1 Cor. 10:13). It is an almost common experience that just when we feel we can take it no longer, divine grace pours into our soul like a ray of light into a dark room. In a posthumous page of Charles Peguy we read:

> Grace is unpredictable, it is shrewd, it is surprising.
> When it does not come directly it comes obliquely.
> When it does not come from the right it comes from the left;
> when it does not come from the left it comes from the right.
> When it is not directy frontal it comes zigzag,
> and when it does not come in a curve it comes in spurts.
> If grace does not come from above it comes from below;
> if it does not come from the center it comes from the circumference,
> and if grace does not come as gushing from a fountain
> it reaches us in a slow stream
> which distills sweetly from the mystical reservoir of Love.

God's Providence oftentimes permits sorrow to enter into our lives as a means of correcting a moral vagary. This bit of Providence, which might be defined as the "divine policy of chiaroscuro," is always accompanied at the right moment with all His help and grace so that we do not succumb on the way.

Another means, seemingly trivial in itself, is truly great for the fruits of patience and interior serenity it produces. It is simply this: to suffer for the love of God. A religious sister related that one of the elderly sisters in her convent, an invalid, had an aspect that was almost transparent. The younger sister asked the sick nun what was the nature of her prayer, that it produced such an effect. The older religious told her: "You see, because I am old and infirm I just whisper this prayer to God: 'Dear God, if it pleases You that I should be like this, I accept it willingly for love of You.... As long as You are content I too am content.'"

At this point it is not difficult to direct our conference to the first source of our patience, that is, to our confidence in God. In the face of suffering we are like the child who looks at the underside of a piece of embroidery: it is all a confusion of threads, and no pattern is discernible; or we are like the tourist who contemplates from the bright outdoors the magnificent stained glass windows of a cathedral: seen from that point of view they reveal no art, no beauty. But if the child observes the right side of his mother's embroidery work he can admire a lovely design in pleasing colors; and if the tourist enters into the gothic cathedral and sees the same windows with the sunshine pouring through, he can contemplate and gaze upon all the scintillating and enchanting scenes of light and harmony. So also at the end of this life we shall be convinced that God was quite right when He chose to permit sorrow to enter our life.

At the risk of overworking our theme we feel that it will be helpful to include here a few lines from a tract on Providence written by St. John Chrysostom, the popular apologist. Thus does the great orator and Patriarch of Constantinople express it:

> Do you doubt Providence? Wait until the end and you will see. Do not get excited, do not become disturbed now. Imagine a person who does not know the trade watching an artist prepare to fuse gold. He sees the artist mixing some ashes and straw. If he does not wait until the end he will think that the poor little piece of gold has been destroyed. Imagine another person, born and reared on the open sea. He suddenly finds himself on solid earth without the least notion of agriculture. If he sees a farmer take grain and throw it to the winds, scattering it on the earth and even

in the mud, he will think that the farmer has wasted the grain and will criticize him. But if that man, before making an unkind judgment about the work of the farmer, would wait for the summer, he would surely change his mind. He would see the field golden with grain, he would see the farmer sharpen his scythe to gather the very grain he had scattered to the winds and left to die. He would see how that grain had multiplied, the grain which seemed lost forever. Now if that farmer has to wait all through the winter, how much more must you wait to the end of the process, considering who it is who plows the land of our soul. And speaking of the end, I am not referring to this present life, but to the future life: the plan of God is directed precisely to our salvation and glory.

This is actual doctrine, valid also for us. In the painful moments of trial we as Christians are called to play the card of trust, trust in God, full and humble trust, without fear, abandoning ourselves to the projects of His love, like the leaf falling from the tree, letting itself be carried wherever the wind will take it. And this is the perfection of patience of which the Apostle St. James speaks (cf. Jas. 1:3-4).

O Lord, You have not promised us blue skies always, or fields in full blossom in every season. Neither have You promised sunshine without rain, victory without wounds, peace without pain.

But You have repeatedly promised us strength for our weakness, light for our darkness, respose for our toil, hope in every desperate situation.

O God, never permit us to be embittered by our lack of success, broken by our sorrow, blinded by our illness so that we do not see Your plan of love.

Supported by Your Spirit, Lord, may we have the grace of knowing how to resist whatever would bring us harm, and how to fight openly and enthusiastically for all that is beautiful, true, virtuous and eternally blessed.

Guide us, O Lord, with Your love and Your providence, and help us always to begin anew with the small or great actions of every day, as steps to arrive at the enjoyment of Your holy embrace.

And all this with Christian patience, unto death, O Lord, for Christian patience is the sign and reward of those who love You!

The Plenitude and the Brilliance of Patience

Patience! A moral virtue believed at first to be one of many, having resemblance to many others! When its unique features have been disclosed, however, it reveals itself as always more beautiful, always more useful and consoling.

In this third part of our exposition we intend to say even more in praise of this virtue, delineating it as the coordinating element of the spiritual equipment of the true follower of Christ, and as the virtue which gives proof of a basic and total adherence of love to the loving will of God.

As impetus and stimulation we offer the example and teaching of the great leaders of Christianity, the Saints.

Synthesis and Marks
of Patience

Differing from the philosophy of Descartes (d. 1650) who advised: "Distinguish to contrast," St. Thomas Aquinas had earlier given the world the very rich philosophical counsel: "Distinguish to unite."

In these pages we shall find a résumé of all our theoretical statements on patience, as well as a review of the manifold practical applications of this virtue to life. They are like many rays of light from one prism, or the vivid colors of one painting. To view them in this way will help us appreciate more fully and taste more vividly this virtue which is so necessary and precious for us in living out our authentic Christian vocation.

St. Cecil Cyprian (210-258), the second writer—following Tertullian—on this subject, eulogizes the virtue of patience in these words:

> This virtue is not restricted to a brief space or to narrow limits; it is poured out and multiplied in many other virtues whose fruits are

derived from the one seed of patience, like many little rivulets springing from the same source. Not one of our actions could be good or could arrive at perfect praise if it were not to draw its title to perfection from this virtue. Patience mitigates the anger in us, it restrains our tongue, it directs our thoughts to good, preserves peace, guarantees discipline; it disarms the attacks of lust, represses the intemperance of pride, extinguishes the flames of enmity. It is the virtue which holds in rein the pretensions of the rich, comforts the miseries of the poor, protects the blissful audacity of virgins, shields the continence of widows, and preserves the reciprocity of love between spouses. Patience keeps us humble in good fortune, strong in misfortune, meek in the face of offense and humiliation. It teaches us to pardon the guilty easily and, if we ourselves have fallen into sin, to persevere in the spirit of penance. Patience makes temptations disappear; it supports persecution, and is perfected in martyrdom. It alone can firmly strengthen the foundations of our hope; it alone can point out the right way of action, following the lead of Christ and setting us in His footsteps to follow on the way of His suffering. It is patience which makes us children of God and shows us how to imitate the goodness of the heavenly Father; it is patience which makes us acceptable to the Lord, reserving for us His infinite mercy.

(From *Tract on Patience*)

St. Zono, Bishop of Verona, preached something similar in the fourth century. This shepherd and major patron of the Venetian city of the Adige, Verona, made some weighty affirmations about this important virtue:

> Patience brings all the virtues into a harmonious unity; without this virtue nothing can be heard or understood or learned or taught. Patience is the one quality to which every other virtue is joined.... Undoubtedly there can exist neither hope nor faith nor justice nor humility nor chastity, neither rectitude nor concord nor charity nor any other spiritual virtue without the mastery and the bridle of patience.... Patience is always ready, humble, cautious, prudent, foresighted, content in every necessity, tranquil in any confusion; its serenity cannot be disturbed by fogs of evil. It escapes the remorse for poorly accomplished tasks, it does not know angry dispute, it averts and supports injustices. Patience seems to be almost immovable no matter what the disturbance, for it remains serene, light, as if nothing contrary had ever happened.... It is well nigh impossible to appreciate the true value of patience, which remains firm and determined despite any difficulty such as fatigue, hunger, nakedness, persecution, fear, danger, death. This virtue—patience—is above hardships, above pleasure, ambition, self-seeking. It remains constant and strong in the glow of almost

divine tempering, and with placid modera-
tion it is able to overcome all the rebellions
of the spirit. If you wish to conquer all with
little effort, first conquer yourself. Your victory consists in this very conquest of
self…"

What St. Augustine (354-430) has to say
on this topic may not be overlooked. Following the example of Tertullian and St. Cyprian,
he too wrote a tract of twenty-nine brief
chapters on the subject of patience. He first
clarifies the usefulness and necessity of this
great virtue, then occupies himself with dis-
tinguishing false patience from true. False
patience, he explains, acts in a purely human
fashion, stoic, almost with the vengeance of
human pride; true patience, instead, draws its
hidden victories from rendering itself like
unto the sufferings of Christ. Beginning with
chapter ten the sainted Bishop of Hippo
presents us with some concrete examples of
patience from the Old as well as the New
Testament; radiant there above all are the
figures of Job and of the martyrs, valiant
models for the inspiration of the people of
God of the New Testament. Then in the
fourteenth chapter, almost reechoing St. Cyprian and St. Zeno of Verona, this son of
Monica speaks of patience as the synthesis of
every virtue, describing it as companion of

divine charity and first source of every good disposition. From here it is easy for Augustine to insist that patience is a very special gift of God, confirming his assertion with a wealth of biblical references. In the closing chapters, the 28th and 29th, the Doctor of Grace and Predestination speaks of patience as a mark of election to eternal life, as the royal road of the heirs to the goods of heaven and as the virtue which gives fullness and secure access to the beatitude of eternal love.

At this point we cannot resist recounting an episode from the life of a great saint, admirable and imitable in his patience, the summit and epilogue of Christian perfection. The story is told in the eighth chapter of the *Fioretti*, the Little Flowers of St. Francis, that one time in the bitter cold of winter St. Francis of Assisi was returning from Perugia to Saint Mary of the Angels. His companion was Brother Leo, who was walking a few paces ahead of him. Francis called out to his companion, "Brother Leo, write down and note carefully that if it were to please God that all Friars Minor everywhere should give a great example of holiness and edification, this would not be perfect joy." The two continued their way for a brief space when Francis called a second time: "Brother Leo, write this too: if all the brethren were able to make the lame walk, crooked things straight, the demons flee, the blind see, the deaf hear, the dumb speak, and even what is greater, the dead rise again after four days, even this would not be perfect joy." A third time the Saint interrupted his journey to say: "Write this, Brother Leo. Even if the Friars Minor knew all languages, knew all sciences, were able to explain the Scriptures, if they had the gift of prophecy and the ability to reveal not only the future but also the consciences of all souls, this would still not be perfect joy." In a fourth interruption Brother Francis addressed the other as "Little Lamb of God," telling him to write that even if all the Friars could speak with tongues of angels, describe the course of the stars, knew the qualities of all the plants and the treasures of the earth, were acquainted with the manners of all birds, all fish, all animals and all men, trees, stones, roots and waters, this would still not be perfect joy. A fifth time Brother Leo was addressed and told to write: "...if the Friars Minor had such a gift of preaching that they could convert all infidels to the faith of Christ, this would not be perfect joy." The story tells us that this continued for a space of about two miles, when finally Brother Leo voiced his own wonder: "Father, I beg you then, tell me wherein is perfect joy."

The answer St. Francis gave is somewhat frightening: "If, when we arrive at St. Mary of the Angels drenched with rain, trembling with cold, bespattered with mud and exhausted with hunger, if then we knock at the convent gate and the porter should rudely ask us who we are, if to our answer that we are two of the brethren he should angrily say, 'It is not true; you are two imposters deceiving the world and taking away the alms of the poor; begone!'; if then he should refuse to open to us and leave us outside exposed to the inclemency of the weather, suffering cold and hunger until nightfall, if we then accept such injustice, cruelty and contempt with patience, undisturbed and without complaint, believing in humility and charity that the porter—who really knows us—is inspired by God to treat us in this manner, write down, O Brother Leo, that this is perfect joy. And if we knock again and the porter comes to drive us away with blows and oaths as if we were vile imposters, saying, 'Get away from here, you wretched thieves! Here you shall neither eat nor sleep. Be off to the hospital!'—and if we accept all this with patience, joy and charity, Brother Leo, write that this is indeed perfect joy. And if we are really so cold and hungry we dare knock a third time, calling the porter and begging him with tears to give us shelter for the love of God, and he should come out even more angry than before and exclaim: 'These bothersome fellows! I shall deal with them as they deserve!' and he should beat us with a knotted stick, throw us upon the ground and roll us in the snow—if we bear all these injuries with patience and joy, recalling the sufferings of our blessed Lord, which we may share for love of Him, write, O Brother Leo, that here, finally, is perfect joy.—And now, Brother, listen to the conclusion. Above all the graces and gifts of the Holy Spirit, granted by Christ to His friends, is the grace of overcoming self and accepting willingly for love of Christ all suffering. In all other gifts of God we cannot glory, seeing that they come from God and not from ourselves, as the Apostle Saint Paul reminds us: 'What hast thou that thou hast not received from God?' AND IF THOU HAST RECEIVED IT, why dost thou glory as if thou hadst not received it?' But in the cross of tribulation and affliction we may glory, as the Apostle says in another place: 'I will not glory save in the cross of our Lord Jesus Christ.' Amen.''

O my Jesus, merciful Love,
Accept my love and compel me to fulfill,
always and in every moment,
Your divine will!
I am convinced, Lord, that to be united with
    You

and to do whatever You desire of me
is the most pleasing, the most precious,
the best gift of my love.
I am convinced that to love You with predilection,
even in difficulties,
is the most honorable, the most worthy and
desirable,
the holiest and sweetest occupation of life!
Mother Speranza

Patience and Hope

Hope is the mother of the sweetness of patience in the face of the unpleasant vicissitudes of life.

If today our humanity is groaning and quivering like a machine with its internal mechanism broken, the chief reason is the absence of theological hope. Instead of placing confidence in God, as in past centuries, man today is depending on social programming and electronic computers. This attitude provides an ever more extensive field for development of interior crises. Without doubt, an existence bracketed between two zeros—the zero of birth and the zero of death—cannot fail to produce undulations in one's spiritual life—agitations, frustrations. We have learned that not a few of our social disturbances, our numerous exhibitions of impatience against someone or something, are in great part the effect of the theological impoverishment of our spiritual horizons.

If we wish to return to a wholesome state of serenity and patience, it is necessary that we recapture the ability to go beyond the limits of time, to place ourselves in the sphere of the eternal, the realm of our joyous longing. There is good sense behind this truth. To say *man* is to say *hope*. Man is the one animal which always looks to surpass itself. Man aspires to something better: his vocation is a continuing tension toward a radical newness. For this reason alone, if he is open to the infinite as a flower is open to the sun, he can remain interiorly satisfied, calm, patient.

Hope is instinctive in every man and gives a foundation to whatever he does. But this virtue is above all the qualifying prerogative of a Christian. A packing-case is a packing-case, whether it is placed in one corner or in another, set on its side or on end; that which distinguishes it and makes it useful is its being filled with good things. So with the follower of Christ: his interior qualification does not derive from his being great or rich, intelligent or ignorant of many things, but only if he is filled with trust in God. He begins to be an authentic follower of Christ, not when he attends to the things he sees, but only when his life is oriented by hope with regard to the invisible realities, to the promises of God. For the Christian, to hope is precisely to give value and poetry to this our history, made up as it is of miseries, failures, mourning and contradictions; to hope means to see and enjoy the divine light which radiates from the city of God, surmounting and beautifying every cloud and every tempest. Pope John Paul II expresses this thought in his own rich words: "Certainly it is difficult sometimes to see the light beyond the darkness, but the true Christian is the one who during the night awaits the smile of the dawn, and during the darkness of Good Friday glimpses the joy and glory of Easter Sunday" (April 12, 1980).

In this sense every Christian could be compared to a swimmer who, defending himself from the violence of the waves, lets these very waves carry him to shore. Our way through life is a hard but sure pathway toward the land where peace reigns as queen.

Here we may make the beautiful observation that Christianity is the land of hope and of life eternal. The action of Christ is an event of total salvation. Christ is complete Savior in every direction and every dimension. He saves in body and in spirit, at the individual level, and the social level; He saves in time and in eternity. This is the meaning of the Greek word *sotér* (Savior: cf. Lk. 2:11); and the corresponding verb *sosein* (to save: cf. Mt.

18:11). Even time has to be saved. It is no longer condemned to be blocked within the finite, but in virtue of the salvific power of the Redeemer it has acquired an eschatological dimension, an opening toward eternity. Therefore, through the efficacious and unifying sacrifice of Jesus and through His resurrection there are no longer two separate and antagonistic lives, the terrestrial and the celestial, but one life only, that which begins in time and flourishes in infinite maturation in the splendor of glory. The hope of eternal life, beyond its being a divine gift, is also the means, condition, and advanced surety in the order of salvation, as we have already mentioned in the chapter on patience and suffering. He who patiently perseveres to the end will be saved (cf. Mt. 10:22).

Lord, I want to be among those who risk their lives for You.
What good is a road, if at the end of it there is not someone I love,
someone waiting for me?

Lord, let me walk toward the good, toward the worthwhile, toward You.
I want to spend my life proclaiming Your Word.
Jesus, You have told me to believe in love, as well in joy as in sorrow, in failure as in victory.

You have often told me to have confidence in
    You,
to entrust myself to You, to Your power:
merciful, provident, wondrous.

Lord, fill me with Your love.
Make me ready for Your stupendous, divine
    adventure,
which consists in living with You, for You, to
Your glory, unto death and for all eternity.
    Amen.

Patience and Joy

In a time of trial, the vision of the reward creates an atmosphere of serenity and forbearance which is the source of constant exultation. Just as the Apostles were filled with most profound joy when they had the certainty that all the past events—shadows, doubts, failure, even to the bloody death of their Master—were but the preamble and path to the resurrection of the Lord, in the same way the Christians of all times have the invincible conviction that there is an eternal life of joy for all the elect of God, and this joy colors all their way through hardships, daily monotony, illness and suffering. St. Augustine says that the death and the resurrection of Christ has divided history in two parts: before Easter, the time of patience, of waiting, of sadness, of sorrows and contradictions; after Easter, a time of glory, of peace, of joy—as premium for the sufferings patiently supported in union with Christ. With a phrase as bright as a sword, St. Paul tells us that "all our sufferings are not to be compared to the future glory which will break upon us" (cf. Rom. 8:18).

An example in a personal key. If I knew that by submitting to a painful surgery I would have the absolute certainty of thereby becoming beautiful, youthful, attractive, filled with new energy—in other words, if I were assured of becoming completely renewed—I would surely desire to have this operation because of its wonderful effects. It is precisely such a vision and hope of eternal joys which transform into joy all our daily trials and sorrows. Don Bosco offers us an appealing example: "Just as the little bird continues to sing in the branches even when the wind begins to blow, because he knows he has wings, so we, too, continue to rejoice even when things are not so easy because of the hope which has been given us in Christ Jesus (cf. Rom. 12:12)."

St. Aloysius wrote a long and touching farewell letter to his mother: "I invoke upon you, my Lady, the gift of the Holy Spirit and consolations without limit.... As St. Paul says, charity consists in rejoicing with those who are joyful and weeping with those who are in tears (cf. Rom. 12:15). Therefore, dear Mother, you must rejoice greatly because through your merit God has shown me where my true happiness is, and has freed me from the fear of losing it. I tell you in confidence, most illustrious Lady, that in meditating on the limitless ocean of divine goodness, my mind gets lost and I cannot grasp how the Lord looks upon my slight and brief effort, urging me with the promise of eternal repose and inviting me to the celestial happiness which until now I have been seeking so negligently. I have shed so few tears to attain it, and yet He offers to me the treasure which is the coronation of great efforts and many tears.

"Illustrious Lady, do not permit yourself to offend the divine goodness by mourning as for a dead person one who is living in the sight of God and who with his intercession can help in your necessities much more than he could in this life. The separation will not be very long. We shall see each other in heaven, and, united with the Author of our salvation, we shall experience unending joys, praising with all the powers of our soul and singing His graces eternally. He takes from us that which He first gave us, only to give it back in a place more secure and inviolable, and to adorn us with those goods which we ourselves would have chosen.

"I have written these things only to obey the promptings of my ardent desire that you, O illustrious Lady, and the whole family, consider my leaving as a joyous event. Continue to assist me with your maternal benediction while I am still on the sea sailing toward the port of all my hopes. I have chosen to write to you to manifest more clearly the love and respect which I as a son owe to my mother.''

Though one cannot always see meaning in history, he can always know that his life has a meaning—the encounter with eternal Love. And in knowing this, one can enjoy the anticipation of peace. In the pocket of an unknown American soldier fallen in the last World War this impassioned note was found:

I have never talked to You, Lord.
But now I feel the need of saying ''Good Morning.''
People have told me that You don't exist, and I believed them.
Last night, all of a sudden, Your heaven appeared to me,
and at once I realized that I have been deceived.
How strange that I had to get involved in this hellish war
to find time to look at You,
and it seems to me I needn't really say anything to You.
I am sure of You.
The zero hour is coming. But since I feel You here so close to me,

I am not afraid at all....
Already I hear the signal. Now, Lord, I must
     go....
You know that I love You awfully much.
I have a feeling that this is going to be a
     terrific battle, Lord.
Who knows? Maybe I will be seeing You
     tonight....
Since up until now I have not been a friend to
     You,
I confess, Lord, I would not be surprised if
     You wait for me first
and meet me near the door....
Look at me, Lord. My tears are falling. I am
     weeping!
Do You understand? Thirty years far from
     You!
But why did I not know You sooner?
Now I must really go. So long, Lord.
How wonderful. Since I have met You, death
     does not frighten me anymore.

How truly are youth and joy of heart a
part of the day-by-day waiting for the invitation: "Sail toward the safe harbor of eternal
life!" But we are not unaware that the joy we
should have may be clouded with the thought
that the access to paradise might be rather
difficult for us poor creatures. But instead of
fearing these dark clouds, why not rather
consider the day of judgment as a gift of
divine mercy?

Heaven, the home country of perfect charity, is the culmination of the great love story on our behalf. The whole of Scripture seems to be a setting forth of this thesis, expressing it in terms that are sufficiently clear. Already in the Old Testament there are to be found luminous and comforting indications of this truth. In the second book of the Maccabees, for example, the account is given of a mother who exhorts her seven sons not to fear martyrdom because eternal joy will be its reward. She addresses the youngest son courageously: "Do not fear this butcher, but prove worthy of your brothers. Accept death, so that in God's mercy I may get you back again with your brothers" (2 Mc. 7:29).* And in the book of Wisdom we find the encouraging assurance: "Those who trust in him will understand truth, and the faithful will abide with him in love, because grace and mercy are upon his elect, and he watches over his holy ones" (Wis. 3:9).*

Likewise, not a few passages of the New Testament require us to look upon the day of judgment as a day of love. St. Paul tells us that the Lord will be a good judge to all those who have looked forward with joy to His coming (cf. 2 Tm. 4:8). We read in the letter to the Hebrews: "Christ...when he appears for a second time, it will not be to deal with sin but to reward with salvation all those who are waiting for him" (Heb. 9:28); and St. James offers the hearty assurance: "The merciful need have no fear of judgment" (Jas. 2:13), and also: "...it was those who are poor that God chose to be rich in faith and to be heirs of the kingdom which he promised to those who love him" (Jas. 2:5).* There is a joyous ring of victory in St. Peter's message as he tells us that we, as the elect of God, have been called to an "inheritance which is imperishable, undefiled, and unfading, kept in heaven for you, who by God's power are guarded through faith for a salvation ready to be revealed in the last time. In this you rejoice..." (1 Pt. 1:3-6).*

This thought is repeated also in the well-known "Letter of Judgment," the title given to the letter of Jude. He exhorts: "but you, beloved, build yourselves up on your most holy faith; pray in the Holy Spirit; keep yourselves in the love of God; wait for the mercy of our Lord Jesus Christ unto eternal life" (Jude 20-21).*

Mainly, though, it is the Apostle St. John who points out the day of judgment as "the moment of love and mercy," confiding to us that "Love will come to its perfection in us when we can face the day of Judgment without fear" (1 Jn. 4:17), for Christ "...shall be with you again, bringing the reward to be given to every man according to what he deserves," for He is "the Alpha and the Omega, the First and the Last, the Beginning and the End" (Rv. 22:12-13).

The ultimate victor, then, is the God of mercy. And paradise is the homeland of the pardoned. This pulsating superabundance of love is set in high relief by St. Alphonsus Liguori with his consoling thought: "The Father, in giving us the Son, did not spare the Son so that we could be spared. Together with the Son He gives us every good thing, every treasure, His very own love, and paradise. Not sparing the Son He has given us all, for all good things are certainly less than the Son" (cf. Rom. 8:32).

Thank You, Lord, for this new day, gift of Your love.

Thank You for Your presence, giving joy to our life.

Thank You for Your Word, which illumines our minds.

Thank You, Lord, for everything You pour into our hearts.

Thank You for the horizons of salvation offered by Your Holy Spirit.

Thank You for the brothers who live with us to form Your family.

Thank You, Lord, for Your mercy which always accompanies us.

Thank You for our Redemption, masterpiece of the Trinity.

Thank You for the divine sonship we received in our Baptism.

Thank You for sacramental Communion through which we are united to You.

Thank You for Mary, Mother of the Church and Mother of Tenderness.

Thank You above all for the promise of paradise, eternal triumph of Your love.

Patience Is an Operation of Love and of Confidence in God

In our search for the deep and hidden spring of joyous patience, we have little difficulty in discerning that true patience, in the broader, more positive and more effective sense of the term, is in the last analysis an unconditional confidence in the goodness and power of our God.

The presence of God in the intricate web of our daily life is a dogma of faith and a focal and vital point of Catholic theology. According to the Apostle St. John, through the Incarnation God has set His tent among men for all time. And as in the desert the Chosen People took the tent with them as they progressed toward the Land of Promise, so does the Lord walk on with us; He goes from place to place with us, He is present with us in all situations no matter how confusing and less than good. But the presence of the Lord remains veiled to us, just as it was hidden to the two disciples of Emmaus, Cleophas and the other, whom tradition names Simon. Though they enjoyed the physical nearness of the Lord they did not perceive the glorious reality. Afterwards, perhaps, at the end of our journey, we, like they, shall be convinced that truly the Lord was always our loving companion. If we were to speak of God in terms of justice, of omnipotence, we would feel as if crushed by the divinity, overwhelmed. But if Love is enshrined as the center, it inverts the relation of our dependence with God: it is almost as if God wished to be dependent upon us.

It is a great social malady that the individual easily gets the feeling of being catalogued. But God catalogues no one. He loves us, He loves us even if we are unworthy, even if we are sinners. If He were to love only those who are kind and good, if He were to love us for the great works we do, if He were to love us for the righteousness we think we have, evidently our relation with Him would be exhausted in the one dimension of justice; and His gratuitous love, His patient and pardoning love, would not shine in splendor. But instead God loves us first even though we are not worthy of His love; in fact, our very ethical and existential poverty is like a new title of preference on the part of the Lord, the "friend of sinners." St. Augustine almost sings this wonderful message: "God loves you even when you do not love Him; He loves you even when you are far from Him. If He loses you He comes in search of you, if you do not know the way He comes to meet you! He coaxes you to take hold of His love." St. Leo the Great, a Tuscan, and a fifth-century Pope, offers this delicate comparison in his reflection on the love of God: "The Lord has given voice to the nightingale so that he can fill with harmony the life of his little ones; He has made of Himself a voice of flesh to enfold us fully in His love." Almost as an embellishment to this thought it is a pleasure for us to add the exclamation of Sören Kierkegaard, the Danish philosopher of Copenhagen:

> Lord, You have loved us first!
> We speak of You as if Your first love had been
>   only once,
> but instead, Your love is continually first, day
>   after day, eternally.
> When I awaken in the morning and raise my
>   spirit up to You,
> You are the first to love me first.
> When I arise at dawn and lift up my spirit
>   and my prayer,
> You are there before me, You have already
>   loved me first.
> It is always so.

We ungratefully speak as if Your first love
    had been only once,
while You, You alone, are the mercy which is
    never failing!

Undoubtedly this divine manner of loving could remain incomprehensible to many.
But love cannot be explained; it is intuitive, it
is tasted—and that is enough. Dante Alighieri
set to verse this problem. He lets his Beatrice
address him as brother and instruct him in
this manner:

> This decree, Brother, is buried to the eyes of
> anyone whose discernment is not mature to
> it, nor is the flame of love.
>
> (Paradise, 7:58-60)

Now is the propitious moment to drop
into the furrows of practical life the many
beautiful and inspirational thoughts which
have been written about the patience of God
and our own response of patience, so that
they may grow and bear the fruits of good
resolutions.

The first practical reflection to be offered
is this: If we wish to enjoy the presence and
the patience of the Lord, who strengthens our
weakness and remedies our frequent reactions of impatience, it is absolutely necessary
to have humility as the basis of our relations
with God and neighbor. True poverty in the

biblical sense is the conviction of our own
radical powerlessness in the light of God, and
in consequence a modest, reserved, and un-
judging attitude toward our neighbor. Scripture tells us that the Lord gives His grace
—that is, His gratuitous love—to those who
are humble (cf. 1 Pt. 5:5). For each one of us
the capacity to perfect ourselves in the love of
God and of patience in the daily demands of
life will be in proportion to our humility.
Patience is the fast train which brings us to
humility, and humility is the final station
where we can meet perfection.

A second resolution could be expressed
as an awareness of the Lord, a response to the
presence of Emmanuel, that is, God-with-us.
If we are busy about hearing and attending to
the Lord present within us we shall not have
too much time to be upset about all that we
cannot change around us and even within
ourselves. The writer Solzhenitsyn, Nobel
prize winner in 1970, writes: "Lord, how
necessary it is for me to live in Your presence!
How easy it is for me to believe in You, even
should my spirit weaken and cease to understand. When intellectual men no longer see
beyond the end of the day and are uncon-
cerned about what they must do tomorrow,
You give me the assurance, Lord, of Your
loving presence and the patient care You take
of me, so that all the doors of evil be closed

and I can walk toward Your kingdom of love, and from there I can send to my brothers some rays of Your goodness...."

A third reflection evolves from the resolution of entrusting ourselves entirely to God. A construction worker in New York, wishing to accustom his son not to be afraid of heights, once took him up the highest skyscraper of the city. When they arrived at the top he grasped his little son and dangled him over the ledge as if he were a flag. When the two came down, the other men asked the lad if he had been afraid. "No," he answered, "I was with my father!" Two categories of people are happy and without complexes: children and saints, the first because they entrust themselves entirely to their earthly father, and the second because they entrust themselves unconditionally to their heavenly Father.

Do not depend upon the tree for your support: it may dry up. Do not support yourself on the wall: it may fall down. Do not count on the support of a friend: he may betray you. Neither place your trust in money: it may be stolen from you. Do not count even on yourself, because you yourself have to go out in search of strength.... But lean on God, entrust yourself to Him: He alone is your vigor, He alone is your Love!

Lord, the world is unfeeling and impatient.
But I, too, am at fault.
How often have I counted on my self-
sufficiency, set myself upon the altar.
Often, Lord, have I shattered what I found,
sullied what I touched,
because I believed myself master of things,
capricious lord of my own life.
How often, Lord, has my patience gone to
pieces
because of my wanting to be somebody else
instead of myself, because of my
wanting to appear more, to be more, to
have more,
without even giving a thought that the only
thing that counts is Your love.
Lord, gather together all that remains of me,
a shattered work of art.
You alone can let me be reborn, can make me
new, resplendent.
Help me, Lord, not to lose the hidden
treasure I have discovered;
grant that my new love for You may make me
gentle, patient with myself
and with life, content only to know that You
are with me and love me forever.

Witnesses to Patience

The Lord is so desirous of being understood and loved as "the God of Patience" that during the centuries He has willed to raise up numerous witnesses and prophets who, through their example and their words, transmit to humanity the joy-giving message of His infinite mercy and indulgence. These great men and women lead the long processions of countless patient souls spending their lives in holiness in the family, in social and community encounters, in religious life.

Witnesses to Patience
in the Old Testament

In the eleventh chapter of the letter to the Hebrews we are shown a great number of witnesses of faith, as sign and extension of the infinite mercy of God and as models and leaders for the countless people who must follow the way of human patience. In the twelfth chapter of the same letter the sacred author uses an intuitively catechetical and pedagogical style to invite us to learn from these heroes how to resemble the patient and merciful Father and Jesus Christ whom He sent.

Abel is the first to inaugurate and consecrate the patience of martyrdom at the hands of his fratricidal brother. After the criminal act God dialogued with Cain, whom He protected despite his crime. This dialogue is already sign and prophecy of divine indulgence. "Cain said to the Lord, 'My punishment is greater than I can bear. Behold, you have driven me this day away from the ground; and from your face I shall be hidden;

and I shall be a fugitive and a wanderer on the earth, and whoever finds me will slay me.' Then the Lord said to him, 'Not so! If any one slays Cain, vengeance shall be taken on him sevenfold.' And the Lord put a mark on Cain, lest any who came upon him should kill him. Then Cain went away from the presence of the Lord, and dwelt in the land of Nod, east of Eden" (Gn. 4:13-16).*

But the one who is outstanding for his confidence in the patience of God is Abraham. Beyond the Oriental mentality and even contrary to its conception of divinity as stern justice and authority, Abraham seeks and counts upon the patience and indulgence of the Lord when the sinful cities of Sodom and Gomorrah are to be destroyed (cf. Gn. 18:22-23). In the twenty-second chapter of the book of Genesis we read how the same Lord tests the sincerity of Abraham in commanding him to immolate his son, Isaac. Abraham reveals his faith and patience in his immediate readiness to carry out the divine command. Later he gives another concrete proof of it in leaving house, land and hearth at the order of the Lord to go to a new country of undefined boundaries. In the story of Abraham we find the example and dynamic of true patience, operative, confident and inspiring (cf. Gn. 12).

And Isaac, prototype of Christ the divine Victim—does he not manifest patience as his father takes him up the mountain and brings him to the altar of immolation?

Likewise the patriarch Jacob is a model of patience for us when with courage and forgiveness he goes to his brother Esau, who has exiled him from his own land. And he manifests even greater patience in offering gifts to his persecuting brother in order to seek a friendly reconciliation.

Could we think of Joseph, son of Jacob, without seeing in him, too, a prophet of divine patience? The inspired book of Genesis recounts the story of Joseph, sold by his own brothers in a locality called Dotan, to Midian merchants. He is taken to the land of Egypt where in time he becomes prime minister of the Pharaoh. Not only does he pardon his brothers when they come to Egypt to find relief from the famine in their own country, but with generous clemency and patience he also furnishes them with provisions (cf. Gn. 37—45).

Another figure highly pleasing to God, in whom divine patience shines brightly and abundantly, is Moses. As a newborn infant he was kept hidden by his parents for three months. Inserted into the family of the Pharaoh and raised to a position of power by his counsel and authority, yet he preferred to be maltreated with his own people, slaves in Egypt, than to live luxuriously at court. When he was forced to flee from the region he retired alone to the desert. But his life of long-suffering and patience does not end here. When the Lord appointed him as guide and liberator of the Hebrews, he had to arm himself with patience for the long journey to the promised land of Canaan. He showed outstanding patience as well with the "stiff-necked people" as with the Most High, continually imploring His appeasement whenever a threat of punishment hung over the people because of their sins against God's goodness. As a lesson for us, God tested this elect servant by making him wait on Mount Sinai for six days before giving him the Law. The summit of the patience of Moses came, however, when as a very old man he who had led the Chosen People through the desert to the very boundaries of the Promised Land had to be content to remain outside; far from his own people, he died alone on Mount Nebo.

The typical example of spiritual patience is, doubtlessly, Job. In this extraordinary personage we find three degrees or three movements of progression toward his trial and the crowning of his patience. First, from an abundance of goods and possessions Job falls into humiliating poverty; secondly, after losing his wealth he loses his health; his body becomes one great wound; and thirdly, to the loss of health there is added the loss of his loved ones. Even his own wife derides him and tries to incite him to rebellion against God (cf. Jb. 2:10). But Job resists, he is patient. In the face of the mocking insinuations of his wife he remains loyal to God, despite some reactions produced more by weakness than by infidelity. The doctrinal scaffolding on which Job builds up his proverbial patience, though it does contain some misconceptions, is made up of these elements: God is the Lord of all, therefore He is free to give or to take away. It is the duty of the creature not to murmur against Him but to accept and bless His will, whatever He ordains. Further: God is the Absolute, the Transcendent. No matter how much one tries to scrutinize or comprehend Him, He remains a mystery, an abyss to our little minds. The fact that we cannot know all the thoughts of God, Job tells us, does not authorize us to conclude that He is mistaken or that He is not managing well (cf. Jb. 36:22-23; 37:23). As a third step, Job takes it on trust that the trials to which the just man is subjected must have a happy outcome, and therefore every trial is a pledge of greater prosperity and more abundant benevolence on the part of the Lord (cf. Jb. 42:1-6). And so it happened. The inspired book of Job tells us that in the end the Lord multiplied Job's possessions, blessed him with sound health and gave him the love of other sons and daughters. We read in the epilogue of the book: "Yahweh blessed Job's new fortune even more than his first one" (Jb. 42:12). It is useful to observe that beneath these verbal photographs of Old Testament exemplars of patience there are some natural reactions which, however, do not lessen the quality of patience. This virtue does not necessarily imply the absence of exterior reactions: patience is not stoic ataraxy nor is it simply good nature. We find that both Moses and Job had their moments of tension, the effects of their fragile creatureliness. Our Lord Himself was once irritated by the scribes and pharisees (cf. Mk. 3:5); and Job even went so far as to say, "May the day perish when I was born!" (Jb. 3:3) The substance of true patience is identified rather with a mentality, an attitude of life through which we accept whatever happens to us as a means of progressing toward our perfection, and we use it as a new insertion into the mysterious plan of God's love for us. It is in this vista that our personality as believers in God is brought to light. According to the standards of the world, the human personality is at its zenith in autonomy, a self-sufficiency in every area: economic, operative, affective, social. In the scriptural sense, however, the authentic religious personality is expressed and fulfilled paradoxically at the moment in which a person entrusts himself totally and confidently to the Lord, his strength, his guide, his faithful and patient companion on the long way of life toward the fullness of eternal joy.

> Blessed is God who lives for ever,
>> and blessed is his kingdom.
> For he afflicts, and he shows mercy;
>> he leads down to Hades, and brings up again,
>> and there is no one who can escape his hand.
> Acknowledge him before the nations, O sons of Israel;
>> for he has scattered us among them.
> Make his greatness known there,
>> and exalt him in the presence of all the living;
> because he is our Lord and God,
>> he is our Father for ever.
>
> (Tb. 13:1-4)*

Witnesses to Patience in the Christian Era

The gallery of holy men and women whose lives give testimony to the patience and benevolence of God becomes highly enriched as we see when we contemplate the models and writers of the New Testament era.

At the head of this bright galaxy of saints is the Blessed Virgin. Who is Mary if not the most excellent creature, through whom came to us in the fullness of time the very epitome of the mercy of heaven? Mary's *Magnificat* is the unique hymn spelling out this divine mercy, this goodness of God invading the whole of the human race and bringing man back into communion with the Trinity. Mary is for us the "Mother of Tenderness" (John Paul II).

Together with Mary and after her come the apostles, the evangelists, and all the disciples of the risen Christ who shared in spreading the Good News of divine love to the world. Let us listen first to St. Paul.

The life of this quite exceptional apostle could be framed in three great panels forming a wonderful triptych. The first would depict Saul, the scrupulous observer of the Mosaic Law, persecuting the Christians at the insistence of a mistaken interpretation of the Law. The second panel would show St. Paul at the Damascus Gate, spiritually overtaken by Christ, converted and set apart for the one paramount design of love. But the true Paul would be represented in the third panel: the apostle of the mercy and patience of God. After his conversion at the Gate of Damascus, he described himself as "one who has obtained the mercy of the Lord" (cf. 1 Cor. 7:25). Then he triumphantly spells out a great message of hope for all sinners: "The saying is sure and worthy of full acceptance, that Christ Jesus came into the world to save sinners. And I am the foremost of sinners; but I received mercy for this reason, that in me, as the foremost, Jesus Christ might display his perfect patience for an example to those who were to believe in him for eternal life. (1 Tm. 1:15-16).* For this reason the Apostle of the Gentiles does not cease inviting his converts to proclaim the message of hope and pardon brought to us by Christ (cf. Ti. 2:14). It is for this reason that he begins not a few of his letters with a hymn of thanksgiving praising the patience and mercy of the Savior, as in the letters to the Romans, the Corinthians, the Galatians, and especially to the Christians of Ephesus and of Colossae. For this very reason, too, Paul traverses the roads of the world, covering on foot about 7800 kilometers, and sailing about 9000 kilometers in a ship. How thoroughly imbued he was with the power of his own statement: "For I am sure that neither death, nor life, nor angels, nor principalities, nor things present, nor things to come, nor powers, nor height, nor depth, nor anything else in all creation, will be able to separate us from the love of God in Christ Jesus our Lord" (Rom. 8:38-39).*

We sense an exhilaration of spirit as we read through the works of some of the first Christian apologists, who also chose as a preferred topic the consoling theme of God's mercy. Tascius Cecil Cyprian—known to us as St. Cyprian, Bishop of Carthage, who was martyred in 258—writes at length of the Lord's persevering kindness:

> Just see how great is the patience of God! He tolerates with longanimity the profanity of the times, the idols fashioned of clay and the sacrilegious rites which detract from His majesty and honor. He makes the day to rise and the sun to shine as well upon the good as upon the wicked. Just see! For the one as for

the other—that is, for the innocent and the guilty—for the devout and the impious, for the grateful and the ungrateful, without any difference, at His divine will the winds blow, the fountains spring up, the grain thrives and produces copious harvest, the vines produce luscious grapes, the trees bear rich fruits, the groves proudly wave green boughs, the meadows are studded with flowers. Yet God continues to be offended by sin. But He restrains His ire; and while it is in His power to inflict punishment He prefers to maintain His tolerant patience, enduring the offense and delaying the chastisement with great clemency, awaiting the time when men, ensnared in error and crime, return penitent in their old age to Him who comforts them with the words: "I take no pleasure in the death of anyone—it is the Lord Yahweh who speaks. Repent and live!" (Ez. 18:32) He invites them to return to Him because He is merciful and kind, patient and good, disposed to change the sentence against sinners. St. Paul reminds them of this very thing: "Are you abusing his abundant goodness, patience and toleration, not realizing that this goodness of God is meant to lead you to repentance?" (Rom. 2:4) The condemnation of the impious and the sinner is not determined until there is absolutely no more possibility of return. The fact that God does not strike immediately is the reason some give for not believing in Him. They do not understand that divine patience can last so long in the face of so many sins!

(St. Cyprian: *De Bono patientiae*)

St. Cyprian anticipates St. Augustine. The Bishop of Hippo wrote an interesting tract on patience, weaving through it all like a shining thread, the ineffable tolerance of the living God for sinners. He describes the construction of the Ark of Noah in the perspective of God's patience. "God invited Noah to construct the ark in a hundred years, that is, through a whole generation, while at the same time he was to preach conversion from sin in order to be saved. The Lord's intention," concludes St. Augustine, "is that of patiently calling us to conversion of heart" *(De Catechizandis Rudibus)*.

In speaking of the parable of the barren fig tree which the owner ordered to be cut down (cf. Lk. 13:6-9), Augustine with his intuitive genius interprets it as a demonstration of the prolonged patience of the Lord. The three barren years are the three stages in the history of salvation: the era of the Mosaic Law, the succeeding age of the time of David, and then the time of grace, beginning historically and irreversibly with the Incarnation of the Son of God, for the purpose of universal salvation (cf. Sermon 72:2).

If Aurelius Augustine is the bard of the patience of the Lord, it is his way of expressing gratitude for his personal joyous experience of it. "What return can I make," he exclaimed, "in exchange for the Lord's mercy to me?... I will love You, Lord, and will render You thanks, and will exalt Your name for You have pardoned me always. If You have made my sins melt away like ice, it has been the work of Your grace and Your mercy.... And if I have not sullied myself with other sins this is also the fruit of Your grace" (Conf. 2:7). It was Augustine who handed down to us this phrase, transparent and splendid as a ray of light: "*Ubi miseri, ibi misericordia,*" that is to say, where there is the misery of man, there shines the mercy of God.

A concluding thought from the early writers and apologists comes from St. Ambrose (330-397), who included in his work *Esamerone* a commentary on creation. In this bit of early Christian literature the Bishop of Milan wrote:

> I give thanks to the Lord our God because He has done a wonderful work in which Love can repose. God created the heavens but did not rest; He created the earth but did not rest; He created the sun, moon, and stars but Scripture does not tell us that He rested after this. But Scripture does tell us that after having created man and woman, the Lord

rested. And the explanation is this: From that moment God rested from His material works to begin a work much more noble, that of pardoning those He had created.

After the year 1000 the term "divine patience" seems to have been combined more forcefully with the charity of the Father and the passion of the Son. As we enter this third gallery of saints we can observe some reflection of this in what appears as a supernatural movement of earth toward heaven.

Let us begin with St. Francis of Assisi (1182-1226), "the greatest saint the Catholic Church has produced in centuries" (Paul Sabatier). This son of Pietro di Benardone and Madonna Pica, usually represented with his glance heavenward and his arms extended to embrace all his brethren, provides us with an ideal model for displaying the immense patience of God for us and what should be our own Christian good will toward all God's children.

In a letter to Fra Leonardo, of a noble and high-stationed family, the Poverello of God expressed these sentiments:

> You are holy, Lord, the one God; You do stupendous things!
> You are strong. You are great. You are the Most High.
> You are the omnipotent King, the Father of heaven and earth.

You are One in Three, Lord of all gods.
You are the Good, the All-Good, the highest
    Good,
O God, living and true!
You are love. You are wisdom and humility.
You are beauty.
You are security. You are our peace. You are
    joy and felicity.
You are patience. You are meekness. You are
    our protector and defender.
You are our strength. You are our refuge.
You are our faith. You are our hope. You are
    our charity.
You are our sweetness. You are our eternal
    life.
O great and amiable Lord, our merciful
    Savior!

The perception and reception of this infinite richness and goodness of God rendered Francis extraordinarily kind, patient and merciful toward his neighbor. Once he said to Brother Leo, "Yes, we cannot stop God from being merciful, as we cannot forbid the sun to shine upon us and warm us with its rays. But different from the sun which gives its light without our having anything to do about it, God has willed, O Brother Leo, that His benevolence pass through the hearts of men.... It depends on each one of us whether or not humanity can enjoy divine mercy."

Involved in this supernatural dynamic of eternal charity, Francis, the restorer of the

Church, powerfully felt the need of giving himself to his brothers, preferably to the most needy, the poorest, the most sinful. The core of his whole apostolic and oblative action is his heart, centered in the very heart of God who is perfect charity and mercy. If he hastened to find the three brigands chased from the little convent of Monte Casale by the brethren, if he manifested an affectionate love for the sick and for lepers, his reason was that in such persons the power of divine friendship can shine more resplendently; if he humiliated himself before sinners it was solely and surely because in them the pardon of the Crucified can triumph more freely. He prayed:

> Lord, make me an instrument of Your peace.
> Where there is hatred let me sow love,
> where there is injury, pardon;
> where there is doubt, faith;
> where there is despair, hope;
> where there is darkness, light;
> where there is sadness, joy.

A well-known spiritual son and follower of St. Francis is St. Anthony of Padua. This twenty-ninth Doctor of the Church, born in Lisbon on August 15, 1195, died in the little convent of Arcella on the periphery of Padua on June 13, 1231. In his rich sermons we find many precious thoughts shining like gems, and most often they emphasize a facet of the mercy of God. One of these treasures tells us: "Like a warm sunbeam coming upon us without detaching itself from the sun, the Lord Jesus comes to us without separating Himself from the bosom of divinity, to let us feel the warmth of His love. He is born a child to make us understand that just as little children quickly forget offenses, He, our Savior, loves to forget our sins." Sometimes, too, this "evangelical Doctor," St. Anthony, speaks eloquently of Mary as the Aurora, which is equivalent to saying that she is intimately bound to the divine Sun, announces it and pours it out upon the earth to fascinate with sweetness and life the history of man.

In a famous sermon given on the sixteenth Sunday after Pentecost, Anthony, the Augustinian-become-Franciscan, expressed these strong words: "The mercy of God fills the world! We all, miserable as we are, have received everything from this mercy. Through divine mercy we are what we are, and without it we are nothing. O God, if You withdraw from me Your mercy, I shall fall into eternal misery. Your mercy is the pillar of heaven and earth. If You move it out of place, everything will go to ruin!"

Anthony, the "saint of the incorrupt tongue," the protector of the poor, the helper in finding lost articles, desired that every

Christian, as adopted son of the Father and follower of Christ, should manifest himself to his brothers as "a chalice of love and as an altar on which burns the flame of mercy."

At the death of St. Anthony, St. Thomas Aquinas (1225-1274) was six years old. This dean of philosophers and Christian theologians presented his tremendous and profound thoughts as rotating around three basic axes: First, the culture preceding the coming of Christ, profane as well as spiritual, was a preparation, a sort of prerequisite to help us understand the design of salvation poured out from the heart of a patient and merciful God. Secondly, history finds its ultimate explanation in the love of the Creator, Redeemer and Sanctifier, that is, in the Triune God, the Beginning and End of every kind of temporal or spiritual process. In the third place, St. Thomas sees in the Church the providential and magisterial instrument of God to lead humanity historically to the fullness of divine life. The Angelic Doctor sees, then, how the Omnipotent has accompanied the spiritual and Christian life of humankind with a long and perennial current of patience and benevolence (cf. Discourse of John Paul II at the University of St. Thomas, Rome, November 17, 1979).

By association of ideas the powerful personality of St. Thomas reminds us of the figure of St. Bonaventure, who died in the same year as did St. Thomas (1274). This "Seraphic and Marian Doctor" was elected superior general of the Franciscan Order in 1257, just 31 years after the death of St. Francis. As a preparation for his weighty office he first betook himself to the rocky heights of La Verna to meditate on his new responsibility. On that sacred mountain, where wind-carved peaks soared like cathedral spires toward heaven, this saint too saw in vision what his spiritual Father Francis had seen, a crucified seraph with six wings. Prompted by this vision St. Bonaventure, citizen of Bagnoregio, wrote a mystical operetta entitled "Journey of the Mind Toward God." In this work he tried to show how divine charity is continually attracting us with the patience and power of grace toward the six steps by which to ascend to perfect communion with God. The six steps are these:

1. the recognition of the love of God in creation
2. the recognition of the love of God in the world of sensation
3. the recognition of the love of God in the human soul as such
4. the recognition of the love of God in the soul in grace
5. knowledge of the existence of God through the intuition of love

6. the intuition that God is love; everything tends toward Him and reposes
in Him as the Supreme Good of life.

Next we come to a triad of Italian saints
who merit the name of missionaries of the
benevolence and patience of God. To be
mentioned first of all is St. Margaret of Cortona, who lived from 1249 to 1297. The Lord
called her and drew her from a life little
attuned to spiritual intimacy, making of her a
"fishnet to catch sinners." A contemporary of
St. Margaret of Cortona was St. Angela of
Foligno, who, like Margaret, was also very
worldly. She was about forty years old when
the Crucified attracted her and she became an
apostle of His mercy. As some of her biographers record, the Lord Jesus said to her,
"My love for you has not been only a joke!"

These two messengers of celestial goodness are complemented, or even over-
shadowed by a third extraordinary woman,
Catherine of Siena, born to the Benincasa
family in the Fontebranda Quarter on March
25, 1347. Her death occurred on April 29,
1380, when she was only thirty-three years
of age. With fine psychological intuition
Catherine throws ribbons of light upon
the way of Christian perfection, preaching
and exalting everywhere the superabundant

power of the love of God manifested in His beloved Son Jesus Christ. This master and apostle of the infinite love of the Savior for humanity delineates it in the expressive and glowing image of a bridge, a symbolic representation anticipating in some way the *Ascent of Mount Carmel* of St. John of the Cross. Over the impassable gulf, cleft by sin and invaded by the swollen river of worldly corruption, divine charity constructs a bridge joining earth with heaven. The bridge is Jesus Christ, both in the figure of His body raised upon the cross, in His teaching, and in His grace. This bridge is the only way for those who desire to arrive at eternal life. This whole inspired metaphor is a great poem of divine patience (cf. Apostolic Letter of John Paul II, *Amatissima providentia*, Sixth Centenary of the Death of St. Catherine).

At the end of the sixteenth century and the beginning of the seventeenth, we find raised up for our admiration and imitation the gentle figure of St. Francis de Sales (1567-1622). He defines the patience of God as "honey" and describes it to us in four dimensions: the goodness of the heavenly Father toward us; the passion of the Son as a mark of His patience in view of our sins, and as an invitation to suffer for His love; the operative patience of the Holy Spirit who enriches and beautifies our souls with divine life, as the sun patiently brings to growth and fruition the flowers and fruits of nature through the days of time; and lastly, our obligation and duty to be patient ourselves, to be humble, calm, tolerant with our defects and with those of others.

We cannot develop here the whole thought of the sainted Bishop of Geneva, so we limit ourselves to one sole consideration relative to the first point. "Be like children," exhorts this Doctor of the Church, "who with one hand hold tight to their father's hand while with the other they gather berries from the bushes along the way. So you, too, while with one hand you gather and manage the things of the world, keep the other hand clasped in the hand of your heavenly Father, turning to Him now and then to see if your business and your occupations are pleasing to Him" (Philothea, III, c 10).

Almost contemporary with St. Francis de Sales is St. Vincent de Paul (1581-1660). This patron of all the works of charity writes in a letter (his 3,089th) his view of the meaning of unlimited confidence in the goodness of God: "The great secret of the spiritual life is in abandoning to God everything we love, in abandoning ourselves to every disposition of His will in our regard, in perfect trust that everything will turn out well for those who love and serve God. When we do this we serve the Lord, but we serve Him according to His designs: we let it happen His way. He will be to us father and mother; He will be our consolation and our virtue, and finally He will be the recompense of our love."

Because of the great bearing of her message on our topic and the abundance of revelations granted to her, we may not pass over in silence the apostle of the infinite mercy of God, St. Margaret Mary Alacoque, the favorite of the Sacred Heart. According to what her biographers record of her she was granted about thirty revelations, the most important of which are the first four. In those moments of grace which the saint experienced from 1673 to 1690, the year of her death, Margaret was patiently taught by Christ Himself to comprehend the full significance of His infinite charity for all men and to diffuse this knowledge through the world.

In 1672 there was born in Tarquinia (a little city in the Italian province of Viterbo) a little girl who at her Baptism was given the name Lucia. It was a name of promise. Like a new Catherine of Siena, Lucia Filippini incessantly proclaimed everywhere the Gospel of God's patience and His pardoning love. The immensity of the divine mercy was brought home to her listeners, among whom were many dissolute women. These she befriended, providing for them a shelter in

Rome near the Trajan Column. The core of all her missionary activity was the ineffable charity of God diffused in the hearts of men. The saint said: "I have no confidence in the love of men, because in giving themselves, creatures become impoverished; but I do not doubt the love of the Lord because in giving Himself He is enriched, and in loving His love is multiplied."

These thoughts induce us to quote what St. Thérèse of the Child Jesus revealed of herself: "I will tell you of my most intimate secrets. Yes, for a long time I have believed that the Lord is more tender than a mother. The mother is always ready to pardon the faults of her little one: God also does this for us. And I am of such a nature that, while fear would hold me back, the love of Jesus lets me not only go forward but even fly. Therefore," continues the Little Flower, "my secret is that of being always happy, of always smiling, as well when I fall as when I do well." This youthful Carmelite thought of her God as "He who is able to make it snow only to give me a little pleasure."

At the first streaks of the dawn of the twentieth century—in 1903—St. Gemma Galgani died in Lucca, at the age of only 26. This soul, living always in the sunlight of God's grace, had this to say: "Lord, Your mercy is the great capital of all my hope.... Great and countless are the miseries I carry about with me. Jesus, remember Your mercy. See, my Jesus, I have such great confidence in You that even if I should see hell opened up and find myself on the very brink, I would not despair; and if I should see heaven closed I would not lose trust in Your mercy, because I confide in You, so pitying, so merciful..." (Ecstasy 1902).

Though the Servant of God Louisa Margarita de la Touche is not yet canonized, it would be sad to omit her from this gallery of witnesses to the merciful love of God. Born in an enchanting castle in Valence, France, in 1868, after a youth exteriorly frivolous if not sinful, she visited the sanctuary of Mont-Martre in Paris at the age of 22. Then she made a prayerful retreat in Paray-le-Monial, spiritual homeland of St. Margaret Mary Alacoque; and in order to be enriched with the treasures of the loving heart of God she entered the Order of the Visitation. Painful vicissitudes brought her to the Piedmont in Italy, where she finally settled in Vische, not far from Ivrea. There she founded the institute "Bethany of the Sacred Heart." While it was the mission of St. Margaret Mary to propagate the infinite love of the Sacred Heart of Jesus for all, Louisa Margarita de la Touche, with divine illumination, dedicated herself to revealing the goodness of the Lord above all to the ministers of worship, the priests. This great soul of God, who said that she had "the sun in her soul," died at the age of 47 on May 14, 1915, at three o'clock on Friday afternoon. Her tomb in Vische, jealously guarded by her spiritual daughters, has become an altar. From the silence of her repose there she continues even now to repeat to the world: "My reason for existing is that I may be a nothing, a feather blown by the wind, a grain of sand carried away by the sea—but this feather, this grain of sand are messengers of infinite Love!"

The visit to this gallery of men and women saints of the Church is already long, but we may not neglect at least a quick glance at the alcoves where we find the four saints of Turin of the nineteenth century: St. Joseph Cafasso, the "patience of God toward priests"; St. Joseph Cottolengo, the "patience of God toward the sick and outcast"; St. Leonard Murialdo, founder of the Congregation of St. Joseph, the "patience of God toward workingmen"; and finally, St. John Bosco, the "patience of God toward youth." This last-mentioned, "father and teacher of boys," has anchored his spirituality in that of St. Francis de Sales, centered as it is in the love of God. With this doctrinal orientation he counteracted the pessimistic theological aberrations preached and divulged in his time by the Jansenists. Don Bosco wanted his boys to feel loved and pursued by God the Father; he wanted them to be attached to the sacraments of the Church and to draw from them the inexhaustible charity of the Son; he desired that his spiritual sons live in grace, that all they did as Christians be accomplished and crowned through their living in vital communion with the Holy Spirit.

To think of St. John Bosco is to recall also the person of St. Mary Domenica Mazzarello, the foundress with Don Bosco of the Institute of the Daughters of Mary, Help of Christians. This saint of Mornese is, in the last analysis, a triumph of the silent and patient love of the Holy Spirit. She entrusted herself entirely to this "sweet Guest of the soul" and followed the Holy Spirit most delicately in all His inspirations, those rising in the interior of her own soul as well as those given to her exteriorly through Fr. Pestarino first, and then Don Bosco.

St. Mary Domenica let the Holy Spirit of God guide her, work in her, and adorn her with virtue. Her unhesitating response to this divine Artist and Producer of sanctity was to remain among her sisters as humble, patient, optimistic, trustful even beyond ordinary human limits. What she saw as important was not so much the post one may occupy in life, but rather the direction given to all one's actions. The loving patience of the Holy Spirit was for her the guide and indicator according to which she lived and did everything that needed to be done.

These very brief reflections on St. John Bosco and St. Mary Domenica bring to mind the one duty of those who belong to the Salesian family, the "Society of Don Bosco." According to the thought of Pope John Paul II, "to be a Salesian means to feel the apostolic thrust, the need to make known to the whole world the love and mercy of the divine Redeemer, especially to those—and there are millions—who have not yet heard of it, to the many youth who, lost and disillusioned in a society which depresses and embitters, are often tempted to despair...." It is necessary, however, that "as Salesians they become apostles in their own environment, animated by sincere affection, humble and merciful, sharing in this way in the joys and sorrows of their brothers..." (John Paul II, Discourse to Students of Salesian Sisters, St. Peter's Square, April 25, 1981).

In these our times there is bright hope and significance in the figure of Don Luigi Orione, beatified by Pope John Paul II on October 26, 1980. Don Orione, "God's Bandit," the Apostle of Providence, had a heart which beat only with love for the Lord and for His brothers. He took very seriously the meaning of divine mercy and the urgent need of putting it into effect. It is told that one evening, under the cover of darkness, at the curb of a street a boy confessed to him that he had killed his own mother. The boy said he was impelled to make this confession because he had been highly impressed by a sermon the holy man had preached in a church, speaking in a touching way about the goodness and patience of the Savior who is "the fullness of mercy." Don Orione looked upon the "three mothers": the Madonna, the Church, and his congregation as three great gifts of the heart of God. His catechesis insisted much on the three "P's": peace, paradise, and *pane* (bread), as the promise and effect of the mercy of heaven. His very sufferings were for him "tidbits of the Lord's goodness." His death, which took place on March 12, 1940, was a total YES to the love of God: his last words were: "I am going.... I am going.... Jesus, Jesus!"

A contemporary of Don Orione is the Servant of God Sr. Faustina Kowalska, who died in 1938 at the age of 33, as did Catherine of Siena and also the Carmelite of Arezzo, Saint Theresa Margaret Redi (1747-1770). The message of Sr. Faustina, silenced for a time by the Sacred Congregation for the Doctrine of the Faith (May, 1959), was later sanctioned and approved by the same Sacred Congregation, with the declaration of April 15, 1971.

This message consists in making known and propagating confidence in "Merciful Jesus." The motto of this daughter of Poland was "*Jesu, ufam Tobie*" (Jesus, I trust in You). She promoted a liturgical feast in honor of the divine Mercy, to be celebrated on the first Sunday after Easter; and through a painting of the likeness of the benign countenance of the Savior she willed to transmit to the world the message of the boundless patience and goodness of the Redeemer.

Lord, I desire that You transform me into Your mercy
that I may be a living image of You,
so that Your infinite mercy, penetrating my heart and my soul,
may be manifested to all people.
Lord, You command me to practice mercy in words, in works.
Help me, Lord, that my eyes...my ears...my tongue...my hands...my feet...
and my heart may always be merciful.
If ever I can do nothing with words and works,
I can still do something to spread Your mercy through prayer.
With it I will be able to reach souls
even where I cannot actually go and do anything.

(Sr. Faustina Kowalska)

We can complete this gallery of "messengers of divine mercy and of divine patience," by meditating, as the last personage, the figure of the Servant of God, Father James Alberione (1884-1971), originator and founder of ten religious families, preeminent among which are the Daughters of St. Paul, apostles of the media of social communication.

Right from the time he was a young priest, Father Alberione entrusted his spiritual and personal littleness to the infinite goodness of the Lord. He wrote about himself in 1949:

"I am happy about my misery because the Redeemer will be better glorified in eternity and the Co-redemptrix will be magnified with Him. I trust that I will be saved only through the divine mercy...." A few years later he again emphasized this interior disposition of his by saying:

"I should narrate a twofold story: the story of divine mercy in order to sing a beautiful 'Gloria in excelsis Deo,' and the humiliating story of my lack of correspondence to the excess of divine charity in order to compose a new 'Miserere'" (cf. Last Document, 1953). Father Alberione felt himself to be, in effect, like a "brush in the hands of a great artist": for the awareness of his poverty of talents and of means, he substituted this full, limitless confidence in the powerful and patient action of the Holy Spirit, who creates marvels in humble persons.

He also preached:

"Yes, God is provident. He has assigned an end to each creature, and being goodness itself He is well disposed towards creatures and towards their end. God could do all by Himself, directly, but He makes use of creatures, providing them with the means necessary to make them participate in the execution of His providential plan of love. The means which the Lord uses to lead us to our end (joy, sorrow, long or short life, etc.) are unknown to us; this is why, most of the time, the wise work of divine Providence remains for us wrapped in obscurity..." (cf. *Introduction to Christian Doctrine*, E.P. 1953).

On November 1, 1900, Pope Leo XIII addressed to the world an encyclical, *Tametsi Futura*, to direct the men of the 20th century towards Christ; and Father James Alberione, illuminated and urged on by the Holy Spirit, made that encyclical a point of departure for leading humanity into contact with the fullness of grace, of love and of mercy, emanating from the Savior, "Way, Truth and Life" (Jn. 14:6). (Cf. Alberione, *Thoughts*, EP 1972.)

Today, to everyone, his ten families, drawing from the Eucharist in its threefold form of Eucharist-word or Truth, of

Eucharist-sacrifice or "Way to the Father," and of Eucharist-Sacrament of Life or love, continue to be the sign and pledge of the indescribable goodness of the Lord.

Such providential families, in imitation of the Apostle of the Gentiles, St. Paul, are, as it were, ten powerful rays of light in the world, which, through the apostolate of the "mass media," radiate the divine Mercy, which has its permanent source and its patient methodology in Christ Jesus, "sun of the universe"! (Cf. *Abundantes Divitiae Gratiae Suae*, text of J. Alberione, EP 1971)

The Help of Prayer

It is logical to think that if we really wish to acquire a fine interior balance, or, as St. Ambrose terms it, a "joyous patience," we must necessarily ask for the grace and strength we need from the Giver of every perfect gift (cf. Jas. 1:17) through prayer, the "anchor in the waves and rainbow in the storm" (Kierkegaard).

We may never forget that grace is a very special gift God bestows on the one who asks for it (cf. Phil. 1:29). God is in Himself infinite, He cannot be taken hold of, but He lets Himself become as finite, reachable, conquerable when in prayer someone cries out to Him for help.

We are very weak because we do not pray, we are deceived because we do not pray, we do wrong and foolish things because we do not pray. Our interior frustrations, too, and our faults, are in great part due to the lack of union with God. A soul who does not know how, does not want to pray is as helpless as a fish out of water, as flaccid as a plant without sunlight. On the contrary, the person who is practiced in prayer and meditation can always find new hope and strength. It is not virtue which creates prayer; it is prayer which creates virtue.

Learning to pray is learning to live. Prayer is discovering freedom, it is grasping the sunlight, it is tapping the reservoir of prudence, it is achieving constancy in good. Prayer is winning spiritual victories in the calm of retreat, conquering hatred, cancelling offenses. Prayer is harmonizing oneself with the peace, the strength and the joy of God in whom everything finishes and re-commences, forever! The prophet Baruch exhorts: "Take courage, my children, and cry to God, for you will be remembered by him who brought this upon you...[he] will bring you everlasting joy with your salvation" (Bar. 4:27, 29).

> Lord, grant that I may surrender myself to Your mercy
> as the leaves of the trees entrust their security to the wind
> in their desire to be carried on high.
>
> Lord, enter my life with Your pardon,
> that my soul may become luminous and smiling
> like the gold-spun waves of the sea.
>
> Lord, pour out upon me Your friendship
> that I may give witness to Your joy,

free as the birds who fly in the heavens
singing their changeless songs.

Lord, hold me always close to You.
And if I should lose my way by confusing
earth's festivities with those of heaven,
grant me the grace of returning to You and
one day finding the heaven
where there will nevermore be confusion but
will always be love!

Also by Valentino Del Mazza, S.D.B.

hardbound $3.00
paperback $2.00
MS0632

hardbound $4.00
paperback $3.00
MA0110

hardbound $5.95 per volume
paperback $4.95 per volume

Cycle A – SC0035; Cycle B – SP0203;
Cycle C – SP0204

Daughters of St. Paul

MASSACHUSETTS
50 St. Paul's Ave., Jamaica Plain, Boston, MA 02130; **617-522-8911.**
172 Tremont Street, Boston, MA 02111; **617-426-5464; 617-426-4230.**
NEW YORK
78 Fort Place, Staten Island, NY 10301; **718-447-5071; 718-447-5086.**
59 East 43rd Street, New York, NY 10017; **212-986-7580.**
625 East 187th Street, Bronx, NY 10458; **212-584-0440.**
525 Main Street, Buffalo, NY 14203; **716-847-6044.**
NEW JERSEY
Hudson Mall—Route 440 and Communipaw Ave.,
Jersey City, NJ 07304; **201-433-7740.**
CONNECTICUT
202 Fairfield Ave., Bridgeport, CT 06604; **203-335-9913.**
OHIO
2105 Ontario Street (at Prospect Ave.), Cleveland, OH 44115;
216-621-9427.
616 Walnut Street, Cincinnati, OH 45202; **513-421-5733; 513-721-5059.**
PENNSYLVANIA
1719 Chestnut Street, Philadelphia, PA 19103; **215-568-2638.**
VIRGINIA
1025 King Street, Alexandria, VA 22314; **703-683-1741; 703-549-3806.**
SOUTH CAROLINA
243 King Street, Charleston, SC 29401; **803-577-0175.**
FLORIDA
2700 Biscayne Blvd., Miami, FL 33137; **305-573-1618; 305-573-1624.**
LOUISIANA
4403 Veterans Memorial Blvd., Metairie, LA 70006; **504-887-7631;**
504-887-0113.
423 Main Street, Baton Rouge, LA 70802; **504-343-4057; 504-381-9485.**
MISSOURI
1001 Pine Street (at North 10th), St. Louis, MO 63101; **314-621-0346;**
314-231-1034.
ILLINOIS
172 North Michigan Ave., Chicago, IL 60601; **312-346-4228; 312-346-3240.**
TEXAS
114 Main Plaza, San Antonio, TX 78205; **512-224-8101; 512-224-0938.**
CALIFORNIA
1570 Fifth Ave. (at Cedar St.), San Diego, CA 92101; **619-232-1442.**
46 Geary Street, San Francisco, CA 94108; **415-781-5180.**
WASHINGTON
2301 Second Ave., Seattle, WA 98121; **206-441-3300**
HAWAII
1143 Bishop Street, Honolulu, HI 96813; **808-521-2731.**
ALASKA
750 West 5th Ave., Anchorage, AK 99501; **907-272-8183.**

CANADA
3022 Dufferin Street, Toronto 395, Ontario, Canada.